LOCOMOTION PAPERS

THE NIDD VALLEY LIGHT RAILWAY

by

D. J. Croft

LABOR OMNIA VINCIT

THE OAKWOOD PRESS

ISBN 0 85361 337 0

Printed by S&S Press, Abingdon, Oxford

First Edition 1972
Second revised and enlarged Edition 1987

Published by
The OAKWOOD PRESS
P.O.Box 122, Headington, Oxford.

Contents

NOTICE IS HEREBY GIVEN, that the Mayor, Aldermen, and Citizens of the City of Bradford have made Application to the Board of Trade for consent, under Section 5 of the Bradford Corporation (Nidd Valley Transfer) Light Railway Order, 1904, to INCREASE the WIDTH in the GAUGE of the NIDD VALLEY LIGHT RAILWAY from 3ft. to 4ft. 8½in.

Any objection to such application may be addressed to the Assistant Secretary, Railway Department, Board of Trade, within fourteen days of the date hereof, and a copy of such objection should be forwarded to me, the undersigned.

Dated this 29th day of April, 1904.

FREDERICK STEVENS, Town Clerk.

Town Hall, Bradford.

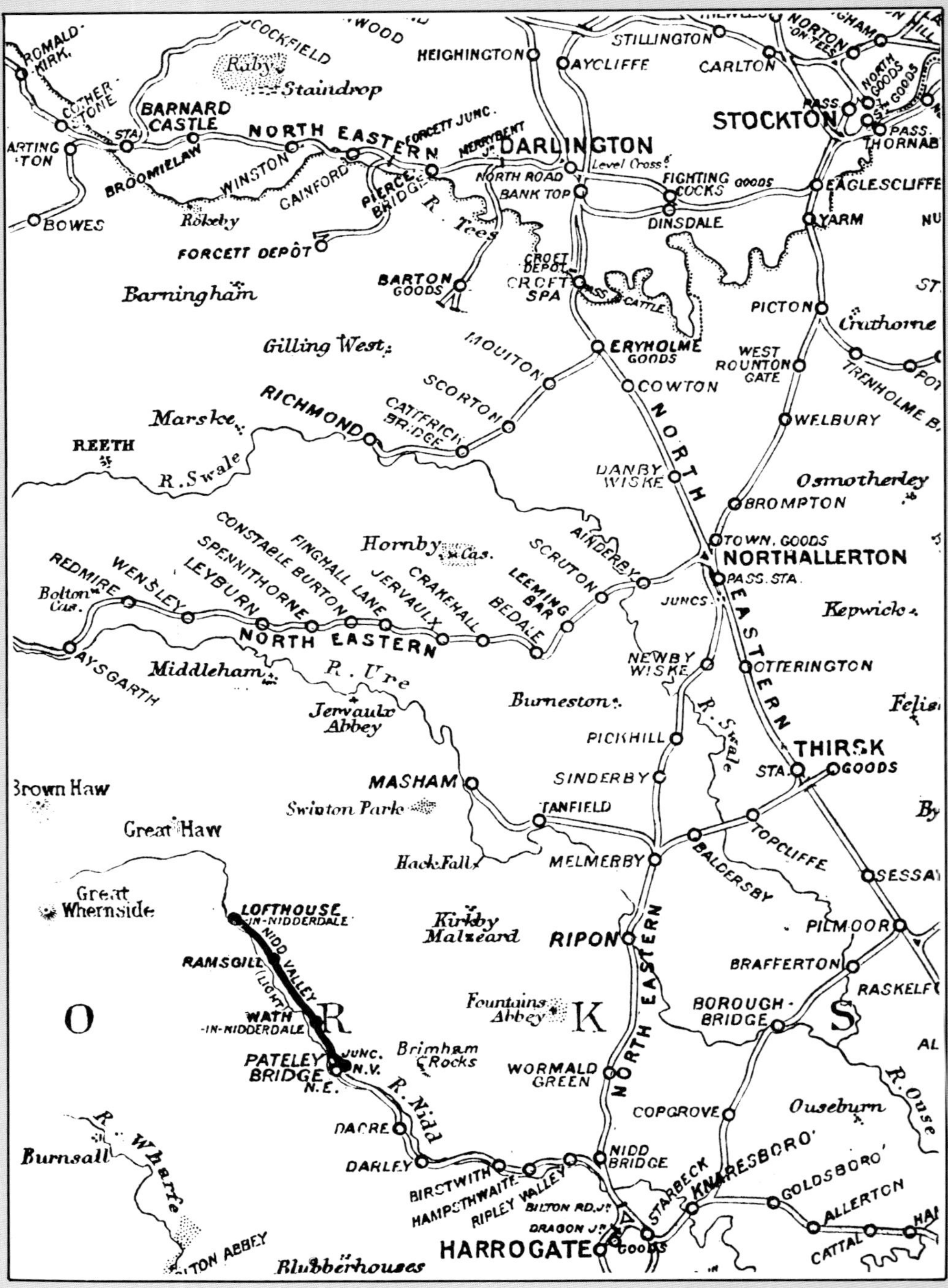

Location map of railway.

The Nidd Valley Light Railway

Introduction

The popularity of the Yorkshire Dales has increased in recent years, visitors from afar being lured by the spectacular scenery portrayed in such television programmes as "All creatures great and small", which dealt with the exploits of a country vet. However, apart from the scenery, there is little today to delight the railway enthusiast, unless he is able to use some imagination and visualise how the valleys looked when the railways played an important part in the life of the dales.

Wensleydale and Wharfedale were served with lines which joined the famous Settle & Carlisle line over to the west. Between these valleys lay Nidderdale which, although having only a terminating branch line, had a far more interesting history, with a branch of the North Eastern Railway, plus one of the lesser-known English Light Railways, the Nidd Valley Light Railway. In the space of thirty years, this unique line came and went, and today the NER branch line to the east is now but a memory also. Railway preservation came too late to save what would have been without doubt a magnificent attraction, but perhaps one day some enterprising group will realise the potential of such a project, and once again lay rails in the Nidd Valley.

The first brief history of the Nidd Valley Light Railway was published by the Oakwood Press in 1972. Since that time, much additional information has been gathered which elaborates the story of this unusual line. As this initial history has been out of print for some years, it was felt that the time had come to re-issue and expand the story, and it is fitting that this new edition should be published fifty years after the closure of the line.

D. J. Croft
January 1987

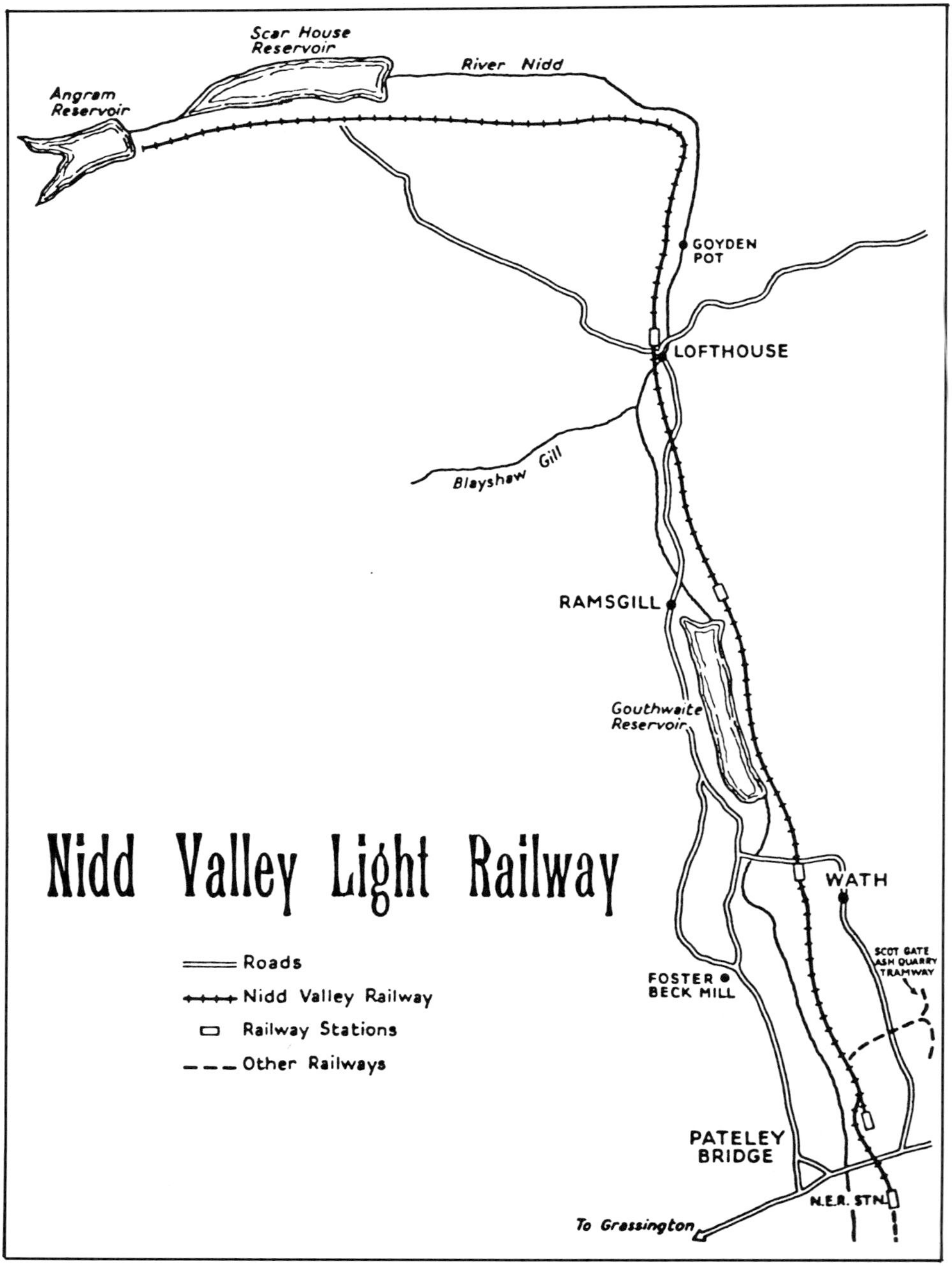
Scar House Reservoir
River Nidd
Angram Reservoir
GOYDEN POT
LOFTHOUSE
Blayshaw Gill
RAMSGILL
Gouthwaite Reservoir
Nidd Valley Light Railway
WATH
Roads
Nidd Valley Railway
Railway Stations
Other Railways
SCOT GATE ASH QUARRY TRAMWAY
FOSTER BECK MILL
PATELEY BRIDGE
N.E.R. STN.
To Grassington

Chapter One

The Origins of the Nidd Valley Light Railway

The valley of the River Nidd is nearly 55 miles long, beginning at Great Whernside, and ending at Nun Monkton, where the Nidd flows into the River Ouse. The area was formerly part of the West Riding of Yorkshire, but since 1974 has been in the County of North Yorkshire. Nidderdale itself is divided into two parts, Upper and Lower, with the market town of Pateley Bridge between the two.

The first substantial historical account of Nidderdale appeared in the Domesday Book of 1086. However, some of the local lead mines were worked in the time of the Brigantes, whilst several surrounding localities suggest Roman occupation. Until the middle of the twelfth century, the area now known as Nidderdale was hunting land with just a few scattered hamlets which belonged either to the King, or to the members of the Mowbray family who owned much of the dale.

Development of local industry

Nidderdale has had several industries over the centuries, notably lead mining, quarrying, and a small textile industry.

Lead mining was a very speculative industry for both the employers and the miners, and the fortunes of the industry fluctuated over the years. From 1550 to 1750 many of the lead-ore veins were well exploited, and an up-turn in the industry a century or so later saw revived interest with several profitable operations in the Upper Nidderdale area. The coming of the railway had a great influence on these operations. The final period of activity in the lead mines took place between about 1914 and 1930, after which the industry finally declined, and today there are numerous reminders in the dale of this once thriving industry.

Stone-quarrying was also a well-established industry in the dale, dating back in parts to the 12th century. The early part of the nineteenth century saw a great increase in quarrying in the valley, the majority of the stone produced being for local use. Once again, the coming of the railway in the 1860s brought about a rapid development in the industry, though now it meant that much stone could be exported from the valley, and several notable London buildings are constructed of Nidderdale stone.

The Nidderdale textile industry dates back to the 13th century, but was associated more with the lower part of the dale. In Upper Nidderdale, the village of Wath had a flax mill by the 1840s, but this was short-lived, though a more successful example was later established at Foster Beck, between Pateley Bridge and Wath. This mill closed early in 1966, after just over a century, the closure being largely due to a shortage of labour, and the need to make expensive repairs to the water wheel.

Having outlined the industrial development of the valley, the reader unfamiliar with these parts should not get the impression of dark, satanic mills and mines, for Nidderdale is an area of outstanding beauty, though being just outside the Yorkshire Dales National Park, it does not receive quite the number of visitors as such places as Skipton or Grassington.

Today, Nidderdale has a new industry – tourism. The increased use of the family car has brought about a complete revival of the whole valley. Pateley Bridge is now a bustling town once again, with attractive shops and ample facilities for the day visitors. An interesting museum was opened in 1975 in premises formerly used by the Rural District Council, and the Nidd Valley Light Railway is well represented, as indeed it should be, for Nidderdale owes it a great debt of gratitude. Without the railway, Upper Nidderdale would have declined, and become one of the forgotten valleys of Yorkshire.

Early railway proposals

It is difficult to imagine that this rural part of Northern England could have had one of the earliest, if not the earliest public railway in the country. In 1818, a local committee was set up in Knaresborough to consider plans for the development of the surrounding area with a view to encouraging local industry. Thomas Telford was commissioned to survey the possible construction of a canal to connect the town with either the River Ouse or the River Wharfe. However, this plan was considered to be too costly, and instead Telford was asked to report on the feasibility of a railway to Knaresborough, which could then be extended to Pateley Bridge to handle the local lead and stone traffic. The report was published in March 1820, but the scheme failed due to lack of support.

More than twenty years were to elapse before any further plans were considered. In 1845, a scheme was published for the building of a railway between Nidd Bridge, on the Leeds to Thirsk line, and Pateley Bridge. Parliamentary approval was granted for this scheme in 1849, but it was decided to postpone the construction of the line until the main line had been extended from Thirsk to Stockton and Hartlepool. This was a major blow to local industry, in particular to the Metcalfe family of Glasshouses. They had invested in the Leeds & Thirsk Railway in the hope that a Nidderdale branch would be built which would benefit their flax mill. As we shall see later, the Metcalfes did not give up hope of a railway link to the valley, but it was to road transport that the local residents were to turn for a solution to their immediate travelling needs.

LIGHT RAILWAYS ACT, 1896.

NIDD VALLEY LIGHT RAILWAY ORDER, 1901.

ORDER

MADE BY THE

LIGHT RAILWAY COMMISSIONERS,

AND MODIFIED AND CONFIRMED BY THE

BOARD OF TRADE,

AUTHORISING THE CONSTRUCTION OF A

LIGHT RAILWAY IN THE RURAL DISTRICT OF PATELEY BRIDGE, IN THE WEST RIDING OF THE COUNTY OF YORK, FROM PATELEY BRIDGE TO LOFTHOUSE.

Presented to both Houses of Parliament by Command of His Majesty.

LONDON:
PRINTED FOR HIS MAJESTY'S STATIONERY OFFICE
BY DARLING & SON, LTD., 34-40, BACON STREET, E.

And to be purchased, either directly or through any Bookseller, from
EYRE & SPOTTISWOODE, EAST HARDING STREET, FLEET STREET, E.C.,
and 32, ABINGDON STREET, WESTMINSTER, S.W.;
or OLIVER & BOYD, EDINBURGH;
or E. PONSONBY, 116, GRAFTON STREET, DUBLIN.

1902.

[Cd. 646.] *Price* $2\frac{1}{2}$*d.*

Public transport comes to Nidderdale

From 1st August, 1849, residents of Nidderdale were able to travel by horse bus from Pateley Bridge to Ripley, to connect with trains on the Leeds & Thirsk Railway. This service was operated by the "Nidderdale Omnibus", though the name of the proprietor is not stated on the locally-printed handbills. The service, which operated twice a day, Sundays excepted, left Pateley Bridge at 7.00 am and 3.00 pm, returning from Ripley at 9.15 am and 6.00 pm. The journey was by way of Wilsill, Smelthouses, New York, Dacre Banks, Dacre, Darley, Burnt Yates, Shaw Mill, Clint, Wreaks and Ripley. The fares for the journey were 1*s.* 6*d.* (7½p) outside, and 2*s.* 0*d.* (10p) inside. Little else is known about the service, but it was presumably withdrawn when the railway did eventually reach Pateley Bridge in 1862.

The railway reaches Pateley

In 1854, when the North Eastern Railway was formed by the amalgamation of several private companies, a deputation of Nidderdale businessmen approached the new company to seek assurances that the Nidderdale branch line would be built. These assurances were given, but it was not until 1859 when those concerned agreed to raise half the capital required that any real progress was made. This amounted to £40,000.

A committee was set up to manage the negotiations, and this consisted of representatives of the main business interests in the valley, as follows:

Messrs Ingilby, Greenwood and Yorke, representing the land owners,

Messrs Hutchinson, Burnaby and Yorke, representing the lead-mining industry,

Messrs John and George Metcalfe and Messrs Francis Thorpe & Company, representing the flax industry.

Construction work on the line began in September 1860, and the 11½ mile line was opened to traffic on 1st May, 1862. The line was single track throughout with intermediate stations at Ripley, Birstwith and Dacre Banks. Subsequently, further stations were added at Darley and Hampsthwaite. The contractors were Messrs Cail & Towns of Newcastle-upon-Tyne, and it is estimated that the line cost around £8,000 per mile.

Finally, after almost half a century, the scene was set for the Nidd Valley Light Railway, though there were to be many obstacles to be overcome before the first train was ready to depart in 1907.

Chapter Two

The Building of the Railway

Bradford's search for water

Towards the end of the last century, the demand for water in the town of Bradford was so great that many additional reservoirs had to be built to provide the water needed to satisfy the domestic and industrial consumers. Bradford had grown at a phenomenal rate – in 1841 the population was 66,713 and by 1891 it had reached 216,361, an increase of 150,000 in just 50 years. The reason for this increase was the thriving textile industry which had developed in the nineteenth century.

The attentions of the Waterworks Committee wisely turned to locating additional sources of water which would provide supplies well into the twentieth century. The valley of the River Nidd, some 40 miles north-west of Bradford provided an ideal location, and between 1893 and 1936 three enormous reservoirs were constructed, which still provide the bulk of the city's water supply to this day.

The Nidd Valley Scheme was promoted in 1890, and in that same year Parliamentary Powers were obtained to intercept the waters of the River Nidd by constructing a reservoir at Gouthwaite, between Pateley Bridge and Ramsgill. Construction work began on 30th September, 1893, and was completed in 1901. The resulting reservoir covers 327 acres, and contains 1,600,000,000 gallons. The total cost of the land and construction work was £240,000. The stone for the reservoir dam was obtained from an adjacent hillside some 500 yards from the dam, and therefore no large-scale railway system was required, though a narrow gauge wagonway was built to bring the stone down to the construction site.

The Nidd Valley Railway is conceived

Around the turn of the century, the inhabitants and land-owners of Upper Nidderdale became interested in the provision of a railway from Pateley Bridge to the head of the Nidd Valley at Lofthouse, a distance of some 6 miles. One of the principal advocates of this new line was John Hawkridge Metcalfe, the eldest son of the late John Metcalfe, who had been one of the original supporters of the branch from Ripley to Pateley Bridge.

In 1900, a syndicate representing the people of Nidderdale sought permission from the Light Railway Commissioners to build the line. Power & Traction Ltd, of Bridge Street, Westminster, London were granted the necessary authority on 30th March, 1901 to construct a 2ft 6in. gauge line from Pateley Bridge to Lofthouse. As originally conceived, the line would carry both passengers and goods, using

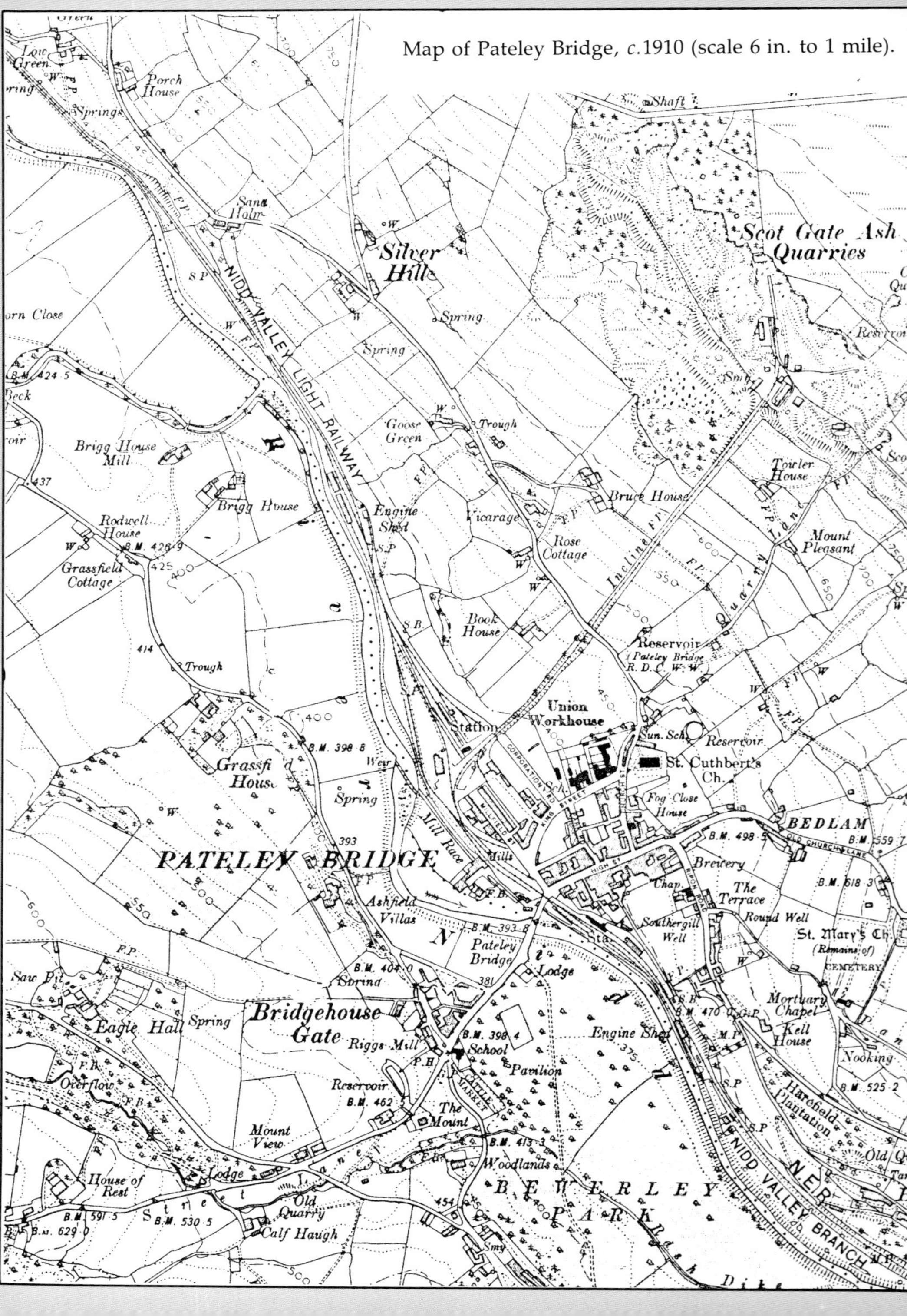

Map of Pateley Bridge, *c.*1910 (scale 6 in. to 1 mile).

steam power over track weighing 35 lb. per yard. The capital involved was £56,000 with powers to borrow a further £12,000 by mortgage.

Power & Traction Ltd had various transport interests including the Aldershot tramways, and plans for a 2ft 6in. gauge steam tramway from Oakington to Cottenham in Cambridgeshire. In addition to the Nidd Valley Railway, they also hoped to build a 3½ mile 3ft 6in. gauge electric tramway from Ripon to Studley Royal, not far from Nidderdale, under the title of the Ripon & District Light Railway Company, but this plan was to come to nothing. Perhaps the tramway schemes were mooted by Mr A. Greenwood, one of Power & Traction's Directors, who was also Chairman of Greenwood & Batley Ltd of Leeds who were well-known tramway engineers. Greenwood & Batley Ltd had tramway interests in their own right too, with the ownership of the Colne & Trawden Light Railway Company in Lancashire.

No doubt Power & Traction could foresee a great future for their Nidd Valley line, for Bradford Corporation had announced its plans to construct two further reservoirs in the valley, which would result in much rail traffic and considerable revenue. However, they were unable to raise the required capital, and for a time it looked as though the scheme might be abandoned. As it happened, Bradford Corporation was to come to the rescue of the scheme, which resulted in it becoming the first local authority in the British Isles to operate a railway.

The Corporation takes over

The area in which the Corporation planned to build its next reservoir posed several geographical problems, chiefly that of accessibility. Access to the region around Angram was virtually non-existent, and what few isolated sheep farms existed were served by mere cart-tracks. It was therefore evident that road haulage to the site on such a huge scale was out of the question, and the Corporation had looked to Power & Traction's proposal as a possible alternative solution. When the latter sought to dispose of its powers, Bradford Corporation had little option but to adopt the scheme itself, for failure to do so may have placed in jeopardy the whole of its future plans for the Nidd Valley.

The transfer of powers to the Corporation was effected under the Bradford Corporation (Nidd Valley Transfer) Light Railway Order, 1904, which was passed on 1st March, 1904. The cost to the Corporation of this Order was £2,000 which had to be paid to Power & Traction Ltd within a period of three months.

There were, however, two important variations from the original Light Railway Order. Firstly, there was a change in the gauge of the line. Power & Traction had originally proposed a 2ft 6in. gauge, but at a meeting of the Bradford Corporation Waterworks Committee on 8th December, 1903, a resolution was passed that authority be obtained to increase the gauge to 3 ft. However, it was soon realised that it would be beneficial if the gauge was changed yet again, to the standard gauge of 4ft 8½in., which would obviate the transhipment of all the necessary supplies at Pateley Bridge, which would in turn considerably reduce operating costs. As a result, the Transfer Order of 1904 empowered the construction of a standard gauge line.

The second variation in the Order had a more serious implication for the Corporation. This was the insistence that the line be used for the carriage of passengers as well as goods over the first six miles of the route from Pateley Bridge to Lofthouse. The Corporation had no alternative but to comply with this regulation, which claimed another first for the progressive Bradford authority in becoming the first municipal owner of a public railway in Britain.

A ceremonial inauguration

The Corporation lost no time in making a start on their new railway. Wednesday 14th July, 1904 was chosen for the inauguration of both the railway and the new reservoir project at Angram. Around 150 members of Bradford City Council, council officials, and invited guests travelled by train from Bradford to Pateley Bridge, and thence to Gouthwaite Reservoir, presumably on foot. Here, at the northern end of the dam, a short ceremony took place to inaugurate the construction of this unique railway. The Mayor of Bradford was presented with an ebony and silver spade by Alderman Holdsworth, the Chairman of the Waterworks Committee. The spade, which was an accurate replica of a navvy's shovel bore a commemorative inscription on the blade. The Mayor discharged his duties efficiently, and the entire party adjourned to Gouthwaite Lodge, where light refreshments were served. And so, the Nidd Valley Light Railway was under way at last.

However, the day was not yet over for the civic party. When the refreshments were completed, the party boarded horse-drawn carriages for the next leg of the journey which was to take them to a remote hillside known as Syke's Brow, about half a mile south of Lofthouse. Here the party boarded a train on the narrow gauge line which had been constructed by John Best & Sons Ltd, the contractor for the Angram Reservoir project. The train, which consisted of two locomotives and about fifteen navvy wagons specially fitted with seats for the occasion, took them the seven miles to Angram, a journey lasting nearly an hour.

At Angram, the party left the train at a specially constructed platform, over which a Union Jack fluttered. The proceedings were conducted by the Mayor, who introduced Mr John Best, the head of John Best & Sons Ltd. He presented souvenirs to Alderman Holdsworth, the Chairman of the Waterworks Committee, and his deputy, Alderman Milner. Alderman Holdsworth received a model railway truck in silver which was about 15 inches in length, and standing on silver rails. On the bodywork of the truck were engraved the Bradford coat of arms and Alderman Holdsworth's initials. Unfortunately, Alderman Milner was not well enough to be present to receive his gift of a model of a contractor's end-tipping wagon also mounted on silver rails. Both models had been expertly made by Messrs Fattorini & Sons of Bradford, a well-known local firm of gold and silversmiths. Alderman Holdsworth then cut the first sod in the construction of Angram Reservoir. It had then been intended that he should read a review of the Corporation's progressive water undertaking, but he too was not well, and his speech was read for him by Mr Thomas Croft, the Assistant Town Clerk.

To close the proceedings, a luncheon was served in the canteen which had been built on the site for the benefit of the workmen employed on the construction site. The luncheon was attended by no fewer than seven former Mayors of Bradford, plus civic dignitaries from other West Riding authorities. The meal over, the party returned the way they had come, and finally arrived in Bradford from Pateley Bridge by special train at around 8.30 in the evening.

Construction begins

Now that construction of the line was under way, the Corporation's attention turned to the buildings which would be needed to operate the railway. The matter of land had already been dealt with by a Waterworks Negotiating Sub-Committee which had visited Pateley Bridge on 5th January, 1904 to talk to people whose land would be affected by the building of the Nidd Valley Light Railway.

The biggest single item on the list of necessary buildings was stations. In addition to the terminal stations at Pateley Bridge and Lofthouse, there were to be two intermediate stations at Wath and Ramsgill. The tender for all four stations went to Messrs Jeptha Thornton & Son on 4th May, 1905 for the sum of £3,050 16*s*. 6*d*. (£3,050.82½). However, they withdrew from the tender shortly afterwards, and the contract was then awarded to Messrs John Best & Sons for £3,040. All four station buildings were similar in appearance, and were stone-built, and contained living quarters on the first floor for the station master and his family.

The firm of Humphrey & Company won the contract to construct a carriage shed at Pateley Bridge for £548, and four goods sheds, one at each station for the sum of £582.

The locomotive shed at Pateley Bridge cost a mere £189, but its builder is not recorded.

The signalling and telephone system installed on the line is worthy of some mention in detail, as it was certainly more than adequate for a line of its type. The trains were to be controlled by Tyler's electric tablet system which was installed at a cost of £360. As far as signalling was concerned, one signal box at Pateley Bridge, built by Best's for £117 8*s*. 7*d*. (£117.43) was considered sufficient. This was situated just outside the station at Pateley Bridge, and controlled the passenger line in and out of the station platform, the lines to the North Eastern Railway station, and the station sidings. Signalling was also provided on the platforms at Wath for £399 0*s*. 4*d*. (£399.02), Ramsgill for £402 17*s*. 4*d*. (£402.87), and Lofthouse £338 11*s*. 0*d*. (£338.55). This equipment was installed by J.B. Saunders & Company of London. At Wath and Ramsgill the lines controlled were the up and down passenger line and the station loop. In the case of Lofthouse, the signals controlled the down line, the line to Angram, and the station sidings. A telephone system, also installed by Saunders provided a link throughout between Pateley Bridge and Angram at a cost of £490.

So far we have considered solely the section of route between Pateley Bridge and Lofthouse, but it must not be forgotten that the line continued a further six miles or so to the reservoir construction site, and that this was also being converted to standard gauge at the same time. This section was laid at the side of a metalled road which had to be cut out of the hillside in places due to the narrowness of the valley. The road was constructed by Messrs Holmes & King of Liverpool, and today still serves the upper part of the dale. At a point approximately mid-way to Angram, a coaling tower and water tanks were provided to replenish the engines on the arduous climb to Angram.

At Angram, in addition to the village which was established to house the extensive workforce, locomotive and carriage sheds were built to house the contractors' locomotives, plus the necessary workshops and offices associated with the operation of the railway. Coaling and watering facilities were also provided here.

With the construction of the railway in progress, only two major matters remained for consideration – rolling stock and staff.

The North Eastern Railway station, Pateley Bridge. *Lens of Sutton*

Another view of the North Eastern Railway station, Pateley Bridge. The connecting line to the Nidd Valley Light Railway is in the distance.
Lens of Sutton

A close-up view of the station at Pateley Bridge. *Lens of Sutton*

Ready to leave Pateley Bridge station in 1928 (*above*) *Milner* waits patiently, whilst (*below*) *Blythe* receives some last minute attention before departure.
Photomatic Ltd

Wath station *Courtesy Railway Magazine*

Wath station, looking towards Pateley Bridge. *LCGB, Ken Nunn Collection*

Ramsgill station. *Lens of Sutton*

Lofthouse station, looking towards the sidings and goods shed. *Lens of Sutton*

Lofthouse-in-Nidderdale, the terminus of the Nidd Valley Light Railway.
Courtesy Railway Magazine

Lofthouse station in 1907 with two locomotives in attendance.
Courtesy Nidderdale Museum

The steam railcar in superb condition at Lofthouse station. *Lens of Sutton*

The Canteen and Angram platform in the distance. *Lens of Sutton*

A busy scene at Lofthouse station in October 1921. The special was a train taking guests to the inauguration of the work on the Scar House Reservoir project. *Lens of Sutton*

The search for rolling stock

A special sub-committee of Bradford Corporation Waterworks Department was appointed to examine and purchase locomotives and rolling stock for the new line, and tenders were received from 11 British locomotive builders. These tenders varied in price from £941 to £1,602, and in each case the company was required to build two locomotives. Just as the decision was about to be made as to which firm would be awarded the contract, it came to the Corporation's attention that a supply of good second-hand locomotives was available, and it was decided that none of the tenders should be accepted, and that second-hand engines would be purchased instead, at a considerable saving to the Corporation.

The source of supply was the Metropolitan Railway which was in the process of converting its London Underground services from steam to electric power. Two locomotives were examined, and subsequently purchased. They were both 4–4–0 tank locomotives, built by Beyer, Peacock & Co. Ltd, No. 20 in 1866, and No. 34 in 1879. The two engines cost £725 and £625 respectively, and on acquisition by Bradford Corporation, the condensing apparatus was removed, and cabs fitted, the work being carried out by the Metropolitan at their Neasden Works. They were also repainted at Neasden in Metropolitan red livery before being despatched to Pateley Bridge, and it is believed that they travelled under their own power via York to reach their new home. On the Nidd Valley Light Railway they were numbered 1 and 2, and named *Holdsworth* and *Milner* after the Chairman and Vice-Chairman of the line.

At the same time as tenders were advertised for the supply of locomotives, tenders were also issued for the supply of two first class composite carriages, two third class composite carriages, and three third class carriages. Again it was decided not to accept any of the tenders, and to purchase second-hand carriage stock from the Metropolitan Railway. Ten assorted four-wheelers were acquired at a cost of £80 each, and these were also renovated and repainted at Neasden before being delivered to Pateley Bridge.

Strangely, when it came to the purchase of goods rolling stock, new vehicles were decided upon. Two brake vans costing a total of £282, and six open goods wagons costing £373 10*s*. 0*d*. (£373.50) were ordered from Hurst, Nelson & Co. Ltd.

The only other item of rolling stock acquired for the opening of the line was a four-wheeled single deck tramcar saloon which was to be used by members of the Waterworks Committee and other visitors. It was built by Hurst, Nelson and delivered in March 1906, but, after the opening of the line in September 1907, it saw little use, and was returned to its builders around 1910.

Staff and uniforms

Staff are probably the single most important feature of any organisation, and the Corporation had no shortage of applicants when it advertised for the numerous posts on the railway. In one case, there were as many as 13 names on the "short list".

Pride of place went to Mr Albert Pearson, who was appointed engine driver at the wage of £2 per week, which also included a house, light and free coal, plus uniform. His fireman, Mr G. Hockley received £1 10*s.* 0*d.* per week, though without any other benefits. The train guard, Mr H. Whitehead, received £1 5*s.* 0*d.* per week.

Two station masters were appointed – Mr T. Fawcett at Pateley Bridge, at £1 10*s.* 0*d.* per week including accommodation, fuel and uniform, and Mr J.H. Julian at Lofthouse, who received £1 5*s.* 0*d.* per week including accommodation, fuel and uniform. The two intermediate stations at Wath and Ramsgill each had a porter/station master, paid at £1 5*s.* 0*d.* per week plus the same benefits as their colleagues at the terminal stations. Mr L. Farrar took up the job at Wath, whilst at Ramsgill was Mr C.E. Wade. Pateley Bridge station also had a porter, Mr F. Robinson, who received £1 per week for his duties, plus uniform.

The three remaining posts were paid at £1 3*s.*0*d.* per week. These were engine cleaner, Mr C.H. Lee, and platelayers Mr D. Garnett and Mr A. Lockwood.

Mr Fawcett, the station master at Pateley Bridge had the responsibility of seeing that the other employees performed their duties satisfactorily, and he also had the responsibility of ensuring that the trains were properly made up, including the many goods trains which travelled over the line to the reservoir construction sites at Angram and Scar House.

Mr William Thomas Croft (no relation of the present writer) was employed as Secretary to the railway, in addition to his other duties.

Uniform clothing was considered of great importance by the railway, and the well-established firm of Brown, Muff & Co. Ltd of Bradford won the contract to supply the necessary clothing. Suits varied from £3 5*s.* 0*d.* to £1 3*s.* 6*d.*, depending upon rank, whilst overcoats and caps were also provided at costs related to status on the line.

Once the driver, stoker and engine cleaner had been appointed to their jobs, they had to apply for certificates of experience before taking up their duties. Surprisingly, this was done by the Midland Railway at Derby, and not by the North Eastern Railway at York as might have been expected. Perhaps there had been some minor disagreement with the NER, though this is not recorded in the Nidd Valley's correspondence files.

The official inspection

The work of constructing the Nidd Valley Light Railway had progressed so well that, by early in 1906, the line was virtually ready for operation. John Best's locomotive was a regular performer over the line, but it was over a year before the line was finally ready to carry its first passengers. It is not clear what caused such a lengthy delay, but things came a little nearer with the official inspection which took place on 24th July, 1907.

Colonel von Donop, for the Board of Trade, made a detailed examination of the track, and tested the bridges and the signalling equipment. On this occasion, neither the Chairman nor the Deputy Chairman of the railway were able to be present, but the Corporation was represented by the Deputy Lord Mayor, Councillor William Land. He had been connected with the Nidd Valley Waterworks Scheme since its inception back in 1893. Also in the official party were the Bradford Waterworks Engineer, Mr James Watson, and, rather surprisingly, representatives of the North Eastern Railway. These included Mr H. Rudgard, the permanent way engineer, Mr Walter Noble, the district superintendent, Mr J. Hirst, the signalling engineer, and Mr W.H. Watson. The reason why so many NER representatives were present is not known – perhaps they had plans for an eventual take-over of the line.

The Colonel completed his inspection of the line, and offered no serious criticism of its construction. He suggested a few minor alterations, but was most impressed with the use of check rails on the curves, a feature not normally adopted on light railways.

The Board of Trade subsequently gave its official permission for the line to open, and at its meeting on 16th August, the Waterworks Committee decided that the official opening should take place on Wednesday, 11th September.

Before the line was opened, however, a minor disagreement took place between John Best & Sons Ltd, the contractors for the line, and the Corporation. Best's had written suggesting that their locomotives should be allowed to operate the winter passenger service over the line, thus reducing the Corporation's financial involvement. The Corporation declined the offer, though no reason was given in their reply. Perhaps the Corporation was afraid that Best's would eventually plan to take over the entire railway, thus reducing its status as the first municipally-owned light railway.

Chapter Three

The Opening, and Early Years up to 1918

The opening of the line

Finally, the great day arrived, and despite an eight-hour Council meeting the previous night, the City Fathers appeared in holiday mood as they assembled at Bradford's Midland Station for the 9.35 am train to Harrogate, from where they travelled over the North Eastern Railway branch line to Pateley Bridge. Arrival at Pateley Bridge was scheduled for 11.08 am, which left the civic party a mere 7 minutes to leave the station and walk the quarter of a mile to the Nidd Valley terminus. It is not recorded whether the train arrived on time, but even a delay of a minute or two *en route* would have forced the dignitaries to make a quick undignified dash along Millfield Street! A ribbon barred the entrance to the station and, after a somewhat lengthy wait for an official photograph, the Lord Mayor, Alderman Godwin, cut the ribbon and led the party into the station building. Here, the Lord Mayor unveiled a brass plaque on the wall to commemorate the occasion, the inscription being as follows:

NIDD VALLEY LIGHT RAILWAY
Opened by the
RIGHT HONOURABLE The LORD MAYOR
ALDERMAN GODWIN, J.P.
11th September, 1907

MR ALDERMAN HOLDSWORTH, J.P., Chairman
MR ALDERMAN MILNER, Deputy Chairman
FREDERICK STEPHENS, Town Clerk
JOHN BEST & SONS, Contractors
JAMES WATSON, M.INST.C.E.
WM. THOS. CROFT, Secretary

The station was specially decorated for the occasion with bunting and flags, as were the other stations on the line.

The inaugural train consisted of the locomotive *Holdsworth*, three ex-Metropolitan Railway carriages, and the Corporation's private saloon carriage at the rear. The Lord Mayor mounted the footplate of the engine to take control of the train, an event which scored another "first" for the Corporation. At 11.15 am the inaugural train jerkily left the platform, and proceeded on its way to the first station at Wath. Here many alighted, perhaps put off by the Lord Mayor's capabilities as engine driver, and walked the short distance to the reservoir dam. At Gouthwaite Lodge, an hour's halt was made for light refreshments, the train departing on its way again at 12.30 pm. A further halt was made at Ramsgill Station, though for what purpose is not recorded in the press reports of the opening. When the train arrived at Lofthouse, *Holdsworth* was detached from the train, and a contractor's locomotive was substituted for the six mile journey to the reservoir construction site at Angram which was reached at 1.30 pm.

At Angram, a temporary wooden platform had been constructed for the visitors to alight on. A tour of inspection then took place, and lasted almost an hour. The navvies were so busy in their work that it is reported that they did not stop work even for the Lord Mayor. Next on the agenda was a visit to the floor of the construction site, and the official party was lowered down to see the work at first hand, before being raised to the surface.

At 3.00 pm, lunch was served in the Reading Room. Alderman Holdsworth, the Chairman of the Nidd Valley Light Railway, was to have presided at the celebration luncheon, but illness prevented him from taking the chair, though he was well enough to attend. Alderman Milner was absent through illness, which is somewhat ironic as the railway's two locomotives were named after these two dignitaries. Instead, Councillor William Land, the Deputy Lord Mayor, presided over the proceedings.

At the end of the meal Councillor Land proposed two toasts, the first to "The King", and the second to "Queen Alexandra, the Prince and Princess of Wales, and the rest of the Royal Family". The Councillor then proposed a vote of thanks to the Lord Mayor, and presented him with an 18 carat gold medallion depicting one of the line's locomotives, beneath which was the city motto "Labor Omnia Vincit". Councillor Land went on to say that the Corporation were interested in other railways, and that they desired the completion of a line which would put the city in communication with the north and south. He hoped that before long, the citizens of Bradford would have the opportunity of taking part in the opening of another line. At this point there was considerable agreement from the audience, for the "Bradford Through Line", as it had become known, had been the subject of much local discussion for some time. Regrettably, the line was never built, but it was to be only three years or so before the Corporation was to become the owner of a second railway, this time at the Esholt Sewage Works, to the north of Bradford, but this was purely an industrial railway, and did not convey passengers.

In his reply, the Lord Mayor said that not every municipality would have had the pluck to tackle an undertaking like the building of a railway, and he proposed a toast to the "Success of the Undertaking".

Councillor T. Sowden was entrusted with the task of replying to this toast, and he said that all felt proud to think that the Bradford Corporation railway was successfully inaugurated. He gave the Lord

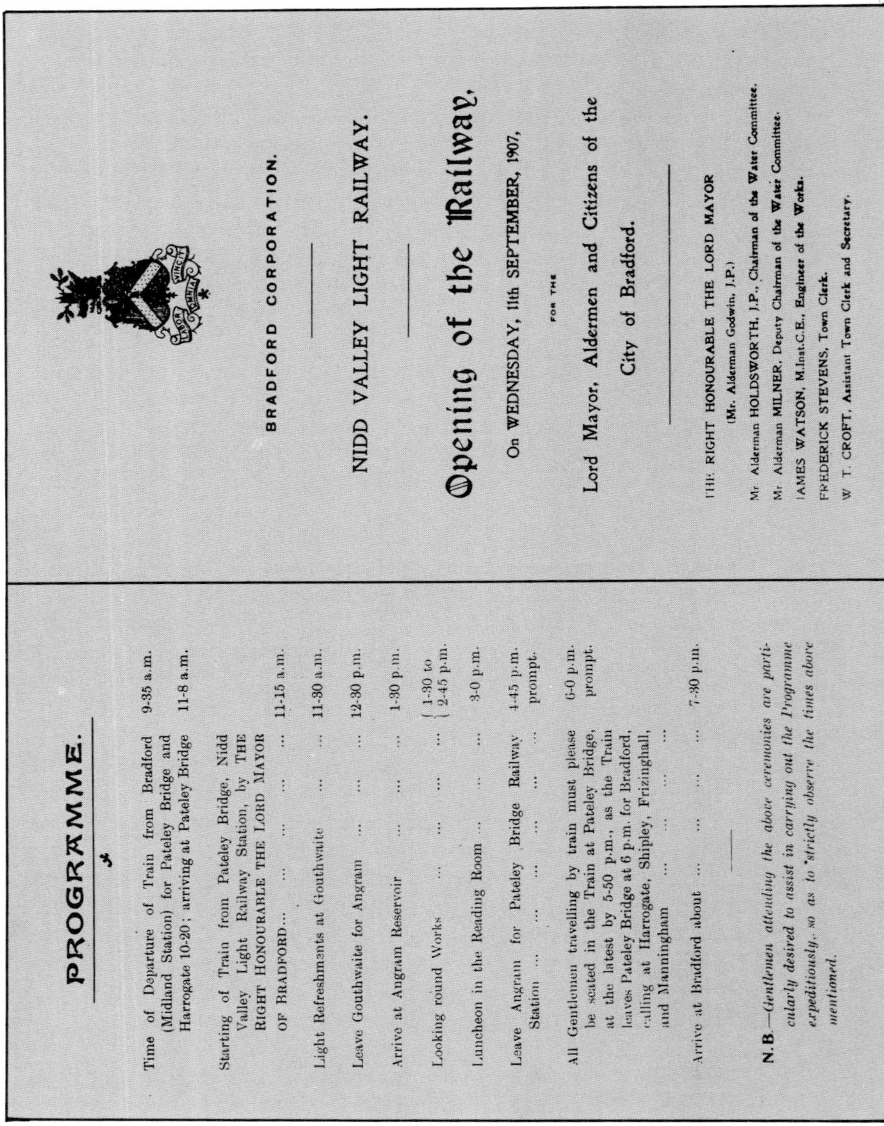

BRADFORD CORPORATION.

NIDD VALLEY LIGHT RAILWAY.

Opening of the Railway,

On WEDNESDAY, 11th SEPTEMBER, 1907,

FOR THE

Lord Mayor, Aldermen and Citizens of the City of Bradford.

THE RIGHT HONOURABLE THE LORD MAYOR
(Mr. Alderman Godwin, J.P.)

Mr. Alderman HOLDSWORTH, J.P., Chairman of the Water Committee.

Mr. Alderman MILNER, Deputy Chairman of the Water Committee.

JAMES WATSON, M.Inst.C.E., Engineer of the Works.

FREDERICK STEVENS, Town Clerk.

W. T. CROFT, Assistant Town Clerk and Secretary.

PROGRAMME.

Time of Departure of Train from Bradford (Midland Station) for Pateley Bridge and Harrogate 10-20; arriving at Pateley Bridge	9-35 a.m. 11-8 a.m.
Starting of Train from Pateley Bridge, Nidd Valley Light Railway Station, by THE RIGHT HONOURABLE THE LORD MAYOR OF BRADFORD	11-15 a.m.
Light Refreshments at Gouthwaite	11-30 a.m.
Leave Gouthwaite for Angram	12-30 p.m.
Arrive at Angram Reservoir	1-30 p.m.
Looking round Works	1-30 to 2-45 p.m.
Luncheon in the Reading Room	3-0 p.m.
Leave Angram for Pateley Bridge Railway Station	4-45 p.m. prompt.
All Gentlemen travelling by train must please be seated in the Train at Pateley Bridge, at the latest by 5-50 p.m., as the Train leaves Pateley Bridge at 6 p.m. for Bradford, calling at Harrogate, Shipley, Frizinghall, and Manningham	6-0 p.m. prompt.
Arrive at Bradford about	7-30 p.m.

N.B.—*Gentlemen attending the above ceremonies are particularly desired to assist in carrying out the Programme expeditiously, so as to strictly observe the times above mentioned.*

Pages from the official programme produced to mark the opening of the line.

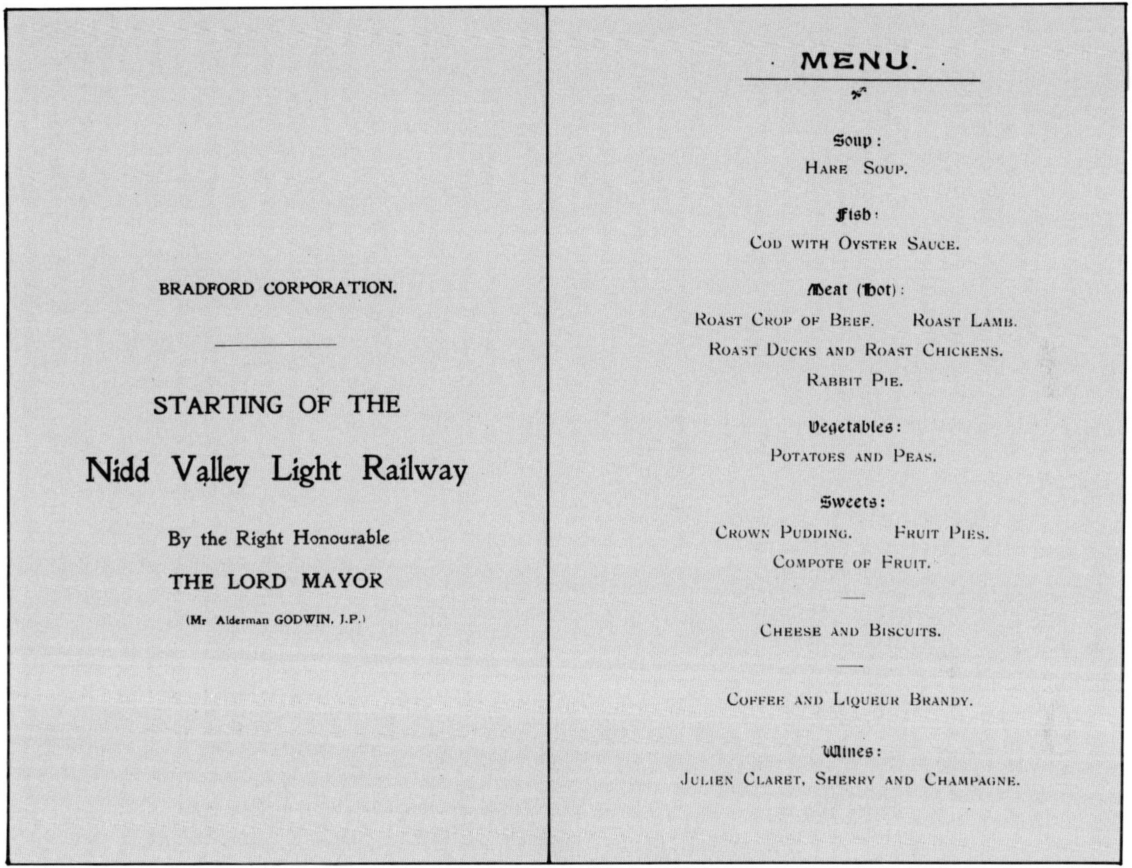

BRADFORD CORPORATION.

STARTING OF THE

Nidd Valley Light Railway

By the Right Honourable

THE LORD MAYOR

(Mr Alderman GODWIN, J.P.)

MENU.

Soup:

Hare Soup.

Fish:

Cod with Oyster Sauce.

Meat (Hot):

Roast Crop of Beef. Roast Lamb.

Roast Ducks and Roast Chickens.

Rabbit Pie.

Vegetables:

Potatoes and Peas.

Sweets:

Crown Pudding. Fruit Pies.

Compote of Fruit.

Cheese and Biscuits.

Coffee and Liqueur Brandy.

Wines:

Julien Claret, Sherry and Champagne.

Mayor credit for his skilful driving of the engine from Pateley Bridge to the end of the line, and expressed a fervent hope that he would take them back as safely!

Other toasts were then drunk to "The Corporation of Bradford", "The Visitors", "The Contractors", and "The Engineer", following which the proceedings ended.

The guest list at this event was quite impressive, including most of the City Council, local landowners, and representatives of both the North Eastern Railway, and surprisingly the Midland Railway.

At 4.45 pm the official party began their return journey, leaving Angram for Pateley Bridge. The final stage of the trip involved a through train from Pateley Bridge to Bradford, departing at 6.00 pm, and calling at Harrogate, Shipley, Frizinghall and Manningham before reaching Bradford at about 7.30 pm. At the end of a long day, the civic party were confident in the knowledge that Bradford had indeed gained a unique civic asset.

Effects of the railway on Nidderdale

Public service on the Nidd Valley Light Railway commenced on Thursday 12th September, 1907, the day after the official opening. Four trains per day were provided in each direction, departing from Pateley Bridge at 8.40 am, 10.20 am, 1.30 pm, and 6.00 pm, these being timed to connect with trains arriving at the North Eastern Railway station. The journey time allowed was 20 minutes for the 6½ miles from Pateley Bridge to Lofthouse. The first class return fare to Lofthouse was 2*s*. 0*d*. (10p), whilst the third class fare was 1*s*. 0*d*. (5p).

The Corporation was not slow to realise the tourist potential of the line, and return excursion tickets were available, offering generous savings on the normal return fares. The third class return excursion fare from Pateley Bridge to Lofthouse was only 9*d*. (4p). These excursion tickets permitted the bearer to break his journey at either of the intermediate stations, and to continue by a later train, thus enabling the traveller to explore some of the scenic attractions of this hitherto inaccessible valley. The Yorkshire historian Harry Speight, in his book *Nidderdale from Nun Monkton to Whernside* published in 1906, remarked that:

> With the opening this year of the railway "up dale" to the romantic region of Middlesmoor, it seems likely that Pateley Bridge will become a great centre of attraction to visitors in the summer season.

The Board of Trade agreed to allow no more than three excursion trains per week to cross from the North Eastern Railway to the Nidd

Valley Light Railway during the month of September 1907, but even this restriction was not to affect the number of visitors who came to the area to see the valley and to ride on the railway. The influx of visitors, many of them from Bradford, brought prosperity to the valley, but Speight seemed to feel that the railway was more of an asset to the locality than a hindrance, for he wrote in his other book *Upper Nidderdale with the Forest of Knaresborough,* also published in 1906:

> While the calm and seclusion of the district around Lofthouse and Middlesmoor will be somewhat broken by the intrusion of the Light Railway in its midst, the facilities of transit will certainly be greatly enhanced.

The railway was also of great value to the residents of the upper part of the dale who could now travel to the shops in Pateley Bridge in some reasonable comfort at all times of the year. It also meant that farmers could deliver goods to and from the Saturday market held at Pateley Bridge. Unfortunately, the railway was no help to the industrial life of the dale, for what little industry there was was situated away from the line of route.

And so it was to the tourist that the line looked for its prosperity. However, this was to lead to a slight disagreement with the North Eastern Railway only a month after the opening of the line. In October 1907 Bradford Corporation approached the NER asking if it could fix a signpost on their station premises directing visitors to the Nidd Valley terminus. The NER considered the matter and wrote back to the Corporation suggesting that a charge of 10s. (50p) per annum be made for this privilege. The Corporation also considered the matter carefully, and replied that 1s. (5p) per annum would be more appropriate. Here the matter rested, and no sign was erected, though one wonders how many visitors would have benefited from such a sign, for the two stations were over a quarter of a mile apart, and were not visible from each other. How many times also did the residents of the town have to direct would-be passengers for Lofthouse along Millfield Street, a street which to all intents and purposes appeared to be a cul-de-sac?

Money troubles are resolved

As originally conceived, the Nidd Valley Light Railway was expected to cost around £30,000 to construct and equip. By May 1908, however, it was evident that this figure was insufficient, and so, Bradford Corporation applied to the Light Railway Commissioners for an Order to increase the amount, and by the time the line was fully equipped, a further £32,726 had been sanctioned. The Order was worded as follows:

Bradford Corporation (Nidd Valley) Light Railway Orders, (Amendment) Order, 1908.

Order amending the Bradford Corporation (Nidd Valley) Transfer, Light Railway Order, 1904.

Whereas by the Nidd Valley Light Railway Order, 1901 (hereinafter called "the Order of 1901"), the Nidd Valley Light Railway Company were authorised to make and maintain the Light Railway (hereinafter called "the railway"), therein described, from Pateley Bridge to Lofthouse in the West Riding of the County of York.

And whereas, by the Bradford Corporation (Nidd Valley Transfer) Light Railway Order (hereinafter called "The Order of 1904"), the power of the said Company with reference to the construction and working of the railway, and otherwise incidental thereto, were transferred to the Lord Mayor, Aldermen and citizens of the City of Bradford (hereinafter called "the Corporation").

And whereas by the Order of 1904, the Corporation were authorised to borrow for the purposes referred to in that Order such sums as might be required, not exceeding 30,000 pounds.

And whereas, the Corporation have proceeded in exercise of the powers conferred upon them by the said Orders, with the construction and equipment of the railway.

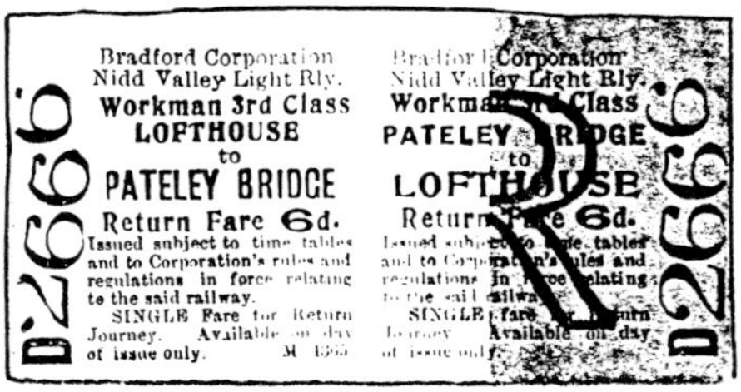

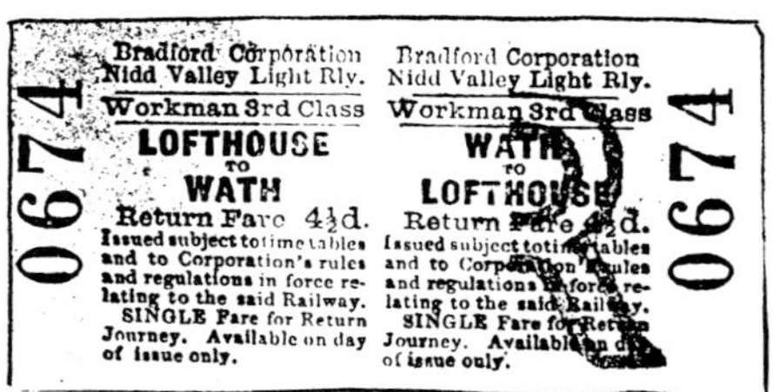

Tickets courtesy Premier Tickets, Leicester

And whereas, the said sum of £30,000 has been found insufficient to meet the expenditure involved in such construction and equipment.

And whereas an application was in May 1908, duly made to the Light Railway Commissioners by the Corporation in pursuance of the Light Railways Act of 1896, for an Order to increase the amount, which by the Order of 1904, the Corporation are authorised to borrow and to extend the period prescribed by the Order of 1904, within which the Corporation shall pay off moneys borrowed by them under the powers of that Order, as amended by this Order, and for other purposes.

By the time the 1908 Amendment Order was granted, the cost of the line was in the region of £55,000 as follows, but the eventual total was closer to £62,000.

		£
1)	Cost of Order and Transfer	2,338
2)	Land	8,149
3)	Construction of the railway	28,630
4)	Telephones, Electric Tablet, Signalling	2,277
5)	Station buildings	2,850
6)	Goods and carriage sheds	1,144
7)	Loco shed	189
8)	Approach roads	670
9)	Rolling stock	3,926
10)	Printing and stationery	1,421
11)	Engineers, Inspectors, Clerk of Works	2,609
		£54,203

Locomotive developments

Apart from one additional staff appointment, the year 1909 was without doubt one of locomotive developments. The appointment of a "strong boy" was approved in February 1909 by the Waterworks Committee. His duties were to assist the station master at Lofthouse, though the name of the successful applicant is not recorded.

Also in February 1909, it was decided that the locomotive *Milner* should be replaced, even though it was the newer of the two ex Metropolitan locomotives, it was nevertheless thirty years old, and was nearly two tons heavier than its shed-mate. Letters were sent to twelve British locomotive builders – Manning Wardle, Hudswell Clarke, Kitson, Thomas Green, Robert Stephenson, Hawthorn Leslie, Andrew Barclay, Beyer Peacock, Brush Electrical, Peckett, Avonside and Kerr Stuart. The specification was for a six-wheeled saddle tank locomotive which would be capable of handling a variety of trains. The contract was awarded to Hudswell Clarke, who duly delivered their completed locomotive (Works No. 882) on 26th May. The new engine took the name *Milner* from the earlier engine, though it was not allocated a number as had been the previous practice.

Doubtless the Corporation was pleased to receive its first brand-new locomotive,but the excitement was short-lived, for it broke down at Ramsgill on 12th June with a blown injection boiler joint. There then commenced a correspondence with the manufacturers, but still the locomotive proved to be troublesome. By August and September, it was constantly out of service, and the Corporation were demanding that Hudswell Clarke send an engineer out to Pateley Bridge to give the engine a thorough check. This seems to have done the trick, for no further trouble is recorded in the line's correspondence file.

At the same time as tenders were invited for the supply of the new steam locomotive, tenders were also invited for a covered auto-railcar seating 40 passengers. Three firms were asked to quote for such an item, these being Bruce Peebles & Company of Pilton Works, Edinburgh; John Milliken of Belfast; and Mountain & Gibson Ltd. Apart from the copies of the letters sent to these builders, there is no further reference in the railway's correspondence so maybe none of the firms was prepared to construct the railcar, or the construction costs were more than the Corporation was prepared to pay. Certainly no such item of rolling stock is mentioned in Corporation records until the acquisition of the Kerr Stuart rail-motor ten years later. However, one source quotes a steam rail vehicle as being in stock in 1910 which adds further to the mystery surrounding this vehicle.

With the entry into service of the new *Milner,* the old locomotive was withdrawn from service and advertised for sale. The Corporation received a letter from the famous Colonel Stephens in May enquiring about the purchase of the withdrawn *Milner,* and offering the sum of £250. Apparently, the Corporation was not prepared to accept this amount, and there the matter rested. Colonel Holman Fred Stephens was well-known in light railway circles as the operator of numerous lines including the Kent & East Sussex Railway, The Weston, Clevedon & Portishead Light Railway, and the Shropshire and Montgomeryshire Railway, and he was also known to be a keen bargain-hunter, especially where second-hand railway stock was concerned. In fact, he already had one ex-Metropolitan 4–4–0T on his West Somerset Mineral Railway, and was obviously keen to acquire another.

After this period of activity early in the year, nothing else transpired for the rest of the year, but 1910 began with another letter from Colonel Stephens enquiring if the line had any surplus locomotives for sale. Presumably the Corporation informed him that old *Milner* was still unsold, and that nothing else was for sale.

The next few years, leading up to World War I, were to prove to be a series of hurdles which the Nidd Valley Light Railway was to overcome, before moving on to a period of more settled existence, though this too was to be short-lived.

Fluctuating fortunes

The period under review, from 1910 to 1914, began with another minor disagreement with the contractors, John Best & Sons Ltd. They had wanted the Nidd Valley Light Railway to install a truck-weighing machine at Lofthouse which would doubtless have saved them a lot of work up at the construction site, but after much discussion, the Waterworks Committee declined to install the machine. It is not recorded what Best's thought of the decision, or whether they built one themselves.

In March 1910 the North Eastern Railway's boiler inspector was asked to examine *Holdsworth,* but it appears to have been over two years before the locomotive was eventually admitted to York Works for repair. The locomotive left Pateley Bridge in May 1912, but was not returned until October of that year, for which the Nidd Valley was charged £213 16*s.* 1*d.* (£213.81). This prolonged non-availability left the passenger service in the sole charge of the new *Milner* which was by now running satisfactorily.

Few statistics relating to the line appear to be available, but a few are known for the year 1910. The total number of passengers carried was 45,344, whilst 13,167 tons of goods were carried. Expenditure during the year amounted to £2,044, whilst receipts totalled £4,137, though no actual profit was made.

In April 1911 the North Eastern Railway wrote to Bradford Corporation to enquire if they would be prepared to allow them to run pleasure trips by charabanc to the Angram site. The Waterworks Department refused to allow the NER's request, stating that they considered their private road from Lofthouse to Angram to be too narrow, as the railway line was laid at the side of the road. Presumably also, they were not keen on another railway company bringing in visitors by road, though it does not seem to have occurred to the Nidd Valley Light Railway to run sightseeing specials which would no doubt have been most lucrative, especially during the summer months. The NER had been a pioneer in running bus services in rural parts of their territory, the first such service having started in September 1903. They also operated a service in Ripon between the railway station and the town centre, and they probably foresaw a chance to use the vehicles at weekends in Nidderdale, which is only about ten miles from Ripon.

The year 1912 was to be one of only two occasions during the railway's history when a profit was made, and then only a meagre £344.

In the space of two years, the Nidd Valley was to lose the two people who had done so much in the early years for the Nidd Valley Waterworks Scheme, and after whom the first two engines were named. Alderman William Holdsworth died on Friday 2nd June, 1911, aged 64. He had been a member of Bradford City Council for over 30 years, and was regarded as the father of the Nidd Valley scheme. He had also become regarded as the permanent Chairman of the Waterworks Committee in recognition of his services. Alderman David Milner, the Deputy Chairman of the Waterworks Committee, died on Saturday 19th April, 1913, aged 75. He had also served on the Council for over 20 years. The name *Milner* was retained on the relatively new Hudswell Clarke 0–6–0, but *Holdsworth* was withdrawn towards the end of 1912, and the name was not perpetuated on any subsequent locomotive.

By 1913 the new *Milner* was requiring a major overhaul, and a long correspondence began with the North Eastern Railway who were asked to do the work at York. By December it had reached the stage where Mr J.N. Smeddle, the locomotive superintendent at York Works, had refused to take the locomotive for repair unless the wheels were removed and the rest dismantled! The Corporation had had enough of this saga, and Hudswell Clarke were asked to do the job instead, and the locomotive was removed to Leeds late in January 1914.

In July 1913 a Mr F.C.C. Jubb of Darlington had written to the railway to see if there were any engines for disposal. The Corporation replied that one was available, though it is not clear which one was offered, but there was no further correspondence, so clearly Mr Jubb was not impressed.

Shortly before World War I broke out, the contract for the telephone system with J.B. Saunders & Company was renewed for a further five years.

The railway in wartime

The outbreak of World War I in June 1914 resulted in the postponement of many vital industrial projects throughout the country, and delay to those which had been started before that time. Angram Reservoir had been under construction for ten years when war broke out, and the work was soon severely hampered by many of the workmen leaving the project to join the war. The Local Government Board instructed all work on the project to stop until the war was over, but Bradford Corporation desperately needed the water, not only for its domestic consumers, but also for the Fire Brigade. The Corporation sent deputations to London, and eventually the work was allowed to continue.

It seems as though the train service on the Nidd Valley Light Railway was unaffected by the war, at least for a time, and four trains continued to run each way. By early 1916, however, the Waterworks Committee were becoming concerned in case the staff required to run the railway should decide to enlist and bring about a temporary cessation of operations. At its meeting on 23rd March, the Chairman reported that an application had been made for exemption from military service of the men engaged on the railway, and that this had been granted on condition that the men remained in their present employment.

Even during the difficult times of 1916, the Corporation was looking to the future, and a decision was taken to supplement Angram Reservoir with another in the Nidd Valley, this time at Scar House. This was to provide a continuing existence for the Nidd Valley Light Railway, which might otherwise have closed on completion of Angram. However, it was not until 1921 that a start was made on Scar House Reservoir, which prolonged the life of the railway still further.

As the war dragged on, it became necessary to curtail the train service, and to introduce mixed trains of passenger and goods stock. Ten days before the war ended, the railway introduced its winter timetable. The service was reduced to three trains per day in place of the previous four. The Corporation made it quite clear that the service would be run as far as circumstances permitted, and that they could not guarantee that the trains would be punctual. In the case of the 10.30 am departure from Pateley Bridge, it was clearly stated that it would run as near to time as possible, but an allowance should be made for the shunting of goods at intermediate stations.

Peace was restored on 11th November, 1918, and the Nidd Valley Light Railway was to embark on the busiest period of its existence, and also the most interesting.

Chapter Four

The Later Years, 1919–1929

A new era begins

In January 1920 a new era began for the Nidd Valley Light Railway with the appointment of Lewis Mitchell, the Corporation Waterworks Engineer as Engineer and Manager of the line. Under him, the line was to develop in many ways, with an almost complete change of rolling stock. In April, only three months into his period of office, the Committee was authorised to arrange for the sale of locomotive *Holdsworth,* and to inspect a light steam locomotive, and two motor railcars which had been offered to the line, and to purchase any or all of them. As it turned out, there were no buyers for *Holdsworth,* and it was finally scrapped at Scar House later in the year.

At a meeting on 7th January, 1920, the Waterworks Engineer was asked to investigate the possibility of electrifying the Nidd Valley Light Railway utilising water power from the Angram Reservoir. He duly prepared a report on the feasibility of the project, but on 31st March he told the Committee that the scheme was economically inadvisable.

The members of the Waterworks Committee visited the railway on 29th May, 1920, and inspected the newly-acquired steam locomotive. It was the first 0–4–0 to be owned, and had been built by Hudswell, Clarke & Company. It was intended to be used specifically on the proposed Scar House Reservoir site, and was named *Gadie,* after the Lord Mayor then in office. The Committee also inspected a steam railcar which had been acquired to operate the passenger service on the line. It had been built for the Great Western Railway in 1905 by Kerr, Stuart & Company, and had only recently been sold to J.F. Wake, a Darlington dealer. It duly entered service in July 1920, and was named *Hill* after Sir James Hill, a former Lord Mayor of Bradford, though it does not appear to have carried nameplates.

In August 1920 a major programme of repairs to the railway commenced. Much of the work was concerned with the section above Lofthouse, for this part had suffered heavily from the traffic to the Angram site, and needed to be rebuilt before the Scar House project could commence. During the reconstruction work, it was decided to straighten out many of the sharp curves on the route, and for this purpose it was necessary to acquire 3 acres of land from local farmers. At one particularly bad curve, a tunnel 180 yards in length was driven through the hillside, though the sharp curve alongside was retained to form a passing loop. Passing loops were also laid near Lofthouse and Woodale.

A minor accident of some sort appears to have happened on the railway on Monday 29th August, 1921, though there is no reference in the local press. The only evidence is contained in the Waterworks Committee minutes, where reference is made to claims against the railway by a Mrs Rowley, and a Mr Levi Wilson, but no further details are quoted.

A sudden decision to close Wath and Ramsgill stations was made in 1921 and, in October of that year, the Waterworks Committee agreed on plans to adapt the buildings for residential purposes at a cost of £100 for each station. The actual date of closure is not known, but the work of conversion of the ground floor offices was completed by September 1922. Henceforth, trains only called at the stations when required. At the same time as the stations were altered, the goods sheds were dismantled and removed to Scar Village, where they were joined together to form a laundry.

The line was now ready to begin its part in the construction of Scar House Reservoir which was to take 15 years to complete.

Scar House developments

Wednesday 5th October, 1921 saw the official start on Scar House Reservoir with the cutting of the first sod. The ceremony was performed by the Lord Mayor of Bradford, Lieutenant-Colonel Anthony Gadie, using a special ebony and silver spade. The civic party had travelled to Nidderdale by special train, and at the conclusion of the ceremony, lunch was served in one of the huts being constructed as part of the workmen's village. At the end of the day, the party returned to Bradford, again by special train.

By 1922 an additional round trip had been added to the pre-war timetable, with slight alterations to timings, which gave a 23 minute journey time to Lofthouse, compared with the previous 25, but the return journey was still timed to take 20 minutes.

During the year 1922/1923 electric lighting was installed in the steam railcar *Hill* at a cost of £182 10*s*. 6*d*. (£182.52½).

The railway's only non-steam locomotive was acquired in 1923. This was a Honeywill 40 hp petrol tractor which was purchased new for £350 in September of that year. Honeywill Brothers was the trading name of the Kent Construction & Engineering Company Ltd of Ashford. The business was established to re-condition a quantity of Motor Rail-built Simplex locomotives which had been built during World War I. The Nidd Valley example was purchased for working in Scar Quarry, but its gauge and actual identity are not known.

Consideration was again given during 1923/1924 to the idea of electrifying the Nidd Valley Light Railway using electricity produced by water power from Angram Reservoir. The Waterworks Committee again reached the conclusion that "it is with regret that, after very exhaustive examination of all the circumstances, one is obliged to admit that, under the most economic conditions of layout, the scheme would not be financially a sound proposition". It was estimated that the scheme would have cost £32,000 including overhead line, rail bonding, and the purchase of the two electric locomotives.

The year 1925 saw the purchase of a new steam locomotive for the Nidd Valley Light Railway. The new arrival was an Andrew Barclay 0–6–0ST, and it took the name *Gadie,* the 1920 Hudswell Clarke 0–4–0ST of that name being re-named *Craven,* after Alderman Craven, the Deputy Chairman of the Waterworks Committee.

It is also believed that 1925 saw an increase in the number of locomotives being used by the contractors on the Scar House Reservoir construction site. Eight additional locomotives are thought to have been added to those already at work, but it is not possible to identify most of those concerned, with the exception of *Stringer* and *Trotter,* which were both purchased from Andrew Barclay that year. At the same time as the engines were purchased, there seems to have been a change in the locomotive-naming policy. Previously, contractors' locomotives were named after World War I personalities, but a change was made, naming them after city council members.

1925 was also a busy year up at Scar House. On 5th June the Waterworks Committee travelled by special train to the site to witness three important stages in the construction work. Firstly, the newly-completed 500 kW steam generating power station was inaugurated. The official party then moved on to set in motion a new concrete mixing plant, the actual ceremony being performed by Alderman Craven. After a short time, the first batch of concrete was prepared, and this was hauled to the dam wall by locomotive *Gadie,* decorated with a Union Jack for the occasion. Not long afterwards, *Gadie* was renamed *Craven* when the larger locomotive arrived from Andrew Barclay.

The early 1920s were to see the beginning of the decline in the railway's passenger traffic, and consequently its revenue, as the following passenger figures illustrate:

Year	*Ordinary Passengers*	*Workmen carried*	*Total*
1921–1922	41,051	106,216	147,267
1922–1923	38,054	24,926	62,980
1923–1924	?	?	61,702
1924–1925	?	?	59,790

The chief reason for the dramatic drop in the number of workmen carried was the completion of Scar House Village. Prior to the completion of the village, many of the workmen had been found accommodation in various parts of the valley, and consequently used the railway to reach their work. The Nidd Valley Light Railway was never a profitable undertaking, and had in fact only once returned a profit – that was in 1912. By the end of August 1924 the total loss on the railway had reached £36,435, the worst year being 1922, with a loss of £4,633. Strangely enough, the year 1924–1925 saw a profit of £1,323, the second and final profit made on the line. An additional contributory factor to the continuing losses on the line was the increasing use of motor transport, both for goods and passengers, and charabanc outings to Scar House must have accounted for much of the decline in traffic. The final scene in the Nidd Valley Light Railway's history was about to be enacted.

The last twelve months

The future of the Nidd Valley Light Railway was sealed at a meeting of the Waterworks Committee on 12th April, 1929. The railway's Engineer was asked to take preliminary steps to arrange the closing of the line. At a meeting two months later on 11th June, the decision was made to close the line and dispose of the rolling stock.

The North Eastern Railway was approached to see if they were interested in acquiring the line, but they replied that it would not be in the interests of the company to do so. They were presumably aware of the falling receipts, and the last year was even worse than before, for only 24,906 passengers were carried during the last nine months of operation. After paying income tax of £552, there was a deficit of £1,825.

Also at the April meeting the Committee discussed the possibility of a reduction in fares to off-set the competition from the Pateley Bridge to Lofthouse bus service. A decision on this matter was deferred, but was finally approved on 2nd July, and implemented immediately. This move had come too late to save the line, however.

In June 1929 it was decided that the locomotive *Craven* should be transferred to the Corporation Gas Department, and a figure of £700 was agreed by the two departments. *Craven* was transferred to its new owners in November 1929.

The date set for the closure of the Nidd Valley Light Railway was Tuesday 31st December, 1929, and the line seems to have closed without any ceremony, and the event does not seem to have been reported in any of the Bradford newspapers, which is a sad end to an undertaking which had served the locality and the citizens of Bradford for over twenty years.

Chapter Five

Passengers No More, 1930–1937

Visitors and unusual cargo

Although the Nidd Valley Light Railway officially closed on 31st December, 1929, it was by no means the end of the line. Certainly, the advertised public service ended on that day, but on 1st January, 1930, and for a further six years, the railway was still very much alive. Traffic changed slightly, as the line was now carrying visitors to the reservoir site, rather than local residents to the school and shops. The volume of freight increased considerably as the work on Scar House proceeded. Numerous organised parties visited the site over the next few years, and details of these visits were often recorded in the "Scar Village" magazine. The following parties visited Scar House in late May and early June 1930, for example:

28th May	–	a party of architects
31st May	–	Bradford Corporation Electricity Dept staff
9th June	–	two private parties led by Bradford Aldermen
12th June	–	Guiseley school children
13th June	–	Skellfield School, Topcliffe
14th June	–	Lady Royde Penny Savings Bank

All these parties travelled by the Nidd Valley Light Railway and, as a result, it was necessary to keep sufficient stock available.

The railway found itself carrying an unusual load during 1932. Late in 1931, it was decided to close the Concert Hall and Recreation Room at Scar House, and it was eventually agreed that they should be moved to Westwood Hospital, Bradford, for further use. As a result, the buildings were dismantled and loaded on to the railway and moved to Bradford, though the actual date of removal is not known.

As the years passed, and Scar House was approaching completion, so the number of visitors declined, only to rise again with the official opening of the reservoir on 7th September, 1936. A severe drought during the summer of 1934 had led to the reservoir being partly used even though it was incomplete.

The sale of the century

With the opening of the reservoir came the end of the railway. For a few months, the railway was used for clearing up the site, but in the Spring of 1937 all that needed to be done had been done, and the remaining parts of the village, vast quantities of equipment, and the Nidd Valley Light Railway itself were advertised for sale by auction.

So much needed to be sold that the auction was arranged to last for three days, from Wednesday, 16th June to Friday, 18th June, 1937.

The auctioneer appointed was Mr J.H. Reid, of Shirlaw, Allan & Company of Hamilton, Scotland.

Scrap dealers and representatives of the big armament firms from London, Birmingham, Lancashire, and the West Country were amongst the 300 strong crowd on the first day of the sale. The reason for such interest in the sale was that Britain's arms programme had sent the price of scrap metal sky-high, and many of the larger firms were keen to get whatever they could. The workshops and much of the equipment used on the construction site was auctioned first, along with part of the railway. *Gadie* was steamed up for potential buyers, and was driven up and down by foreman fitter Billy Lloyd. The engine was sold to a Scottish foundry for £1,030.

Some of the equipment was sold far and wide. An aerial cableway, for instance, was sold to the Channel Islands Granite Company Ltd, and installed at L'Etoc Quarry on the island of Alderney.

The sale of the rest of the railway came towards the end of the week. Eight more locomotives were sold off, including *Milner* (II) and *Allenby* which both went to Sir Lindsay Parkinson, the contractors, the former for £650. *Kitchener* fetched £700, but its new owner is not recorded. The steam railcar *Hill* was sold for scrap, but survived for another 40 years! *Watson* and six of the contractors' carriages were sold to Sheffield Corporation for use on their reservoir railway at Ladybower Reservoir. Much of the track-bed from Wath to Lofthouse was purchased by the local council for the construction of a new road which never materialised.

The sale of the railway attracted a large crowd, including villagers from all over Nidderdale. Many of the men who had worked on the reservoir construction sites were also present to see the sale. When their work in Nidderdale was over, some of them moved to construction projects in Singapore, Africa and Australia.

And so, finally, the Nidd Valley Light Railway was no more. The very last train to run on the line was an unscheduled one run by the contractors during the dismantling of the line, and with this there came to an end the busiest and most prosperous era this part of Nidderdale had seen, or is likely to see.

To conclude the story of the Nidd Valley Light Railway, it would seem fitting to end with a passage from *The Railway Magazine* for September 1937, which seems to describe exactly the atmosphere of Upper Nidderdale some fifty years ago:

> When all this is cleared away, and the last train has gone clanking down the lonely valley, there will be little to show, besides the two towering dams, and the great tranquil lakes, what a hive of industry this bleak and desolate spot once was . . .
>
> By the passing of the Nidd Valley Light Railway, the dwindling company of light railways in this country will be the poorer for the loss of one of its most interesting members.

Chapter Six

A Trip Along the Line

Pateley Bridge to Wath

No account of the Nidd Valley Light Railway would be complete without a description of the route of this interesting line, but as we are unable to travel on the railway today, we will have to content ourselves with an imaginary journey, so let us turn the clock back 60 years to 1926, and catch an early afternoon train from Pateley Bridge.

We have arrived in Pateley Bridge from Harrogate on board an NER train, and need to make our way to the terminus of the Nidd Valley line. Fortunately, we know the way, which is just as well, for there is nothing to indicate that this small Yorkshire Dales market town has a second railway station. Leaving the NER station, we cross the High Street, and for a short distance walk along Millfield Street, parallel to the sidings and track that connects the Nidd Valley Light Railway with the NER. We follow the road round to the right, and continue up the slight rise of King Street, before turning left along Corporation Road which brings us to the station. Shortly before reaching the station, we pass under a low bridge which formerly carried the tracks of the inclined tramway up to the Scot Gate Ash Quarry, now disused since World War I. Once under the bridge, the Nidd Valley station is just ahead to the left.

The station building is set at right angles to the tracks, and is a solid two-storey building of local stone. We purchase our tickets at the booking office, and notice the elaborate bronze plaque erected to mark the opening of the line in 1907.

As we walk on to the platform, an unusual feature is immediately apparent. There are two tracks served by two platform faces, the main departure one being of conventional railway construction, but the other platform which appears to be seldom used is made of wood.

Our train is already in, and as we walk along the platform we see that it is composed of three four-wheeled coaches, at the head of which is 0–6–0T *Milner,* new to the railway in 1909. This loco is a frequent performer on passenger trains, and shares the service with the former Great Western steam railcar *Hill.* To the right of our train is the goods shed and several sidings, whilst ahead we can see the line's only signal box, which controls all movements in the station area.

We take our seats in the leading carriage, and before long the guard's whistle sounds and, with a shrill blast on the engine whistle, we move slowly out of the station. About 150 yards out from the platform end, we pass the signal box on our right, and just beyond, a trailing point on the left brings the line from the North Eastern station and sidings in to join our line. Another 150 yards ahead we see the main carriage sheds and engine shed, on the left and right respectively, our train passing between the two. Outside the engine shed stands *Gadie,* simmering gently between trips on supply trains to the Scar House construction site. Once clear of the carriage sheds, the line runs close to the River Nidd for a short time, before the river bends away from us, leaving a closely-cropped field alongside us. At the end of the field, the river is once again beside us, though this time we are passing not through open country, but along a shelf cut out of the rock with an escarpment to our right. Suddenly, the river swings away from us again, and we are running along an embankment above a field of grazing cows. For a third of a mile, the scene remains equally pastoral to the left, but from the right hand side of our carriage, the hillside rises steeply above us. The train begins to slow down as we approach the first intermediate station at Wath.

Wath to Ramsgill

Wath station had a longer history than any of the other stations on the Nidd Valley Light Railway. It had originally been a farmhouse, but had been converted into an inn in 1895 for the use of the Corporation workmen engaged on the Gouthwaite Reservoir project. Subsequently, it had been rebuilt into the present station building, and closely resembles the other stations on the line.

When originally built, there was a passing loop at Wath, plus two short sidings and a goods depot situated to the rear of the station building. There is some doubt as to how long the passing loop remained, for it is not shown on an Ordnance Survey map of 1910, but appears on photos of the line taken in the 1920s. It may have been reinstated when construction traffic on the line increased in the mid-1920s. When the station was opened it was known as "Wath", but was later re-named "Wath-in-Nidderdale" to distinguish it in railway timetables from Wath-on-Dearne, near Barnsley.

The village of Wath was very small, and at one time had the distinction of possessing two of the smallest places of worship in England.

Our train re-starts from Wath, and immediately crosses the lane, before passing on to a low embankment which stretches for almost half a mile until the dam wall of Gouthwaite Reservoir is reached. The reservoir was opened in 1901, and cost £240,000. It covers an area of 327 acres, and contains 1,610,000,000 gallons of water. The lake is very picturesque, and our train runs along the side of the water for almost its entire length. Beneath the waters, on the far shore, is the site of Gouthwaite Hall, which was demolished before the valley was flooded, and the stones were used to build a new hall nearby. The

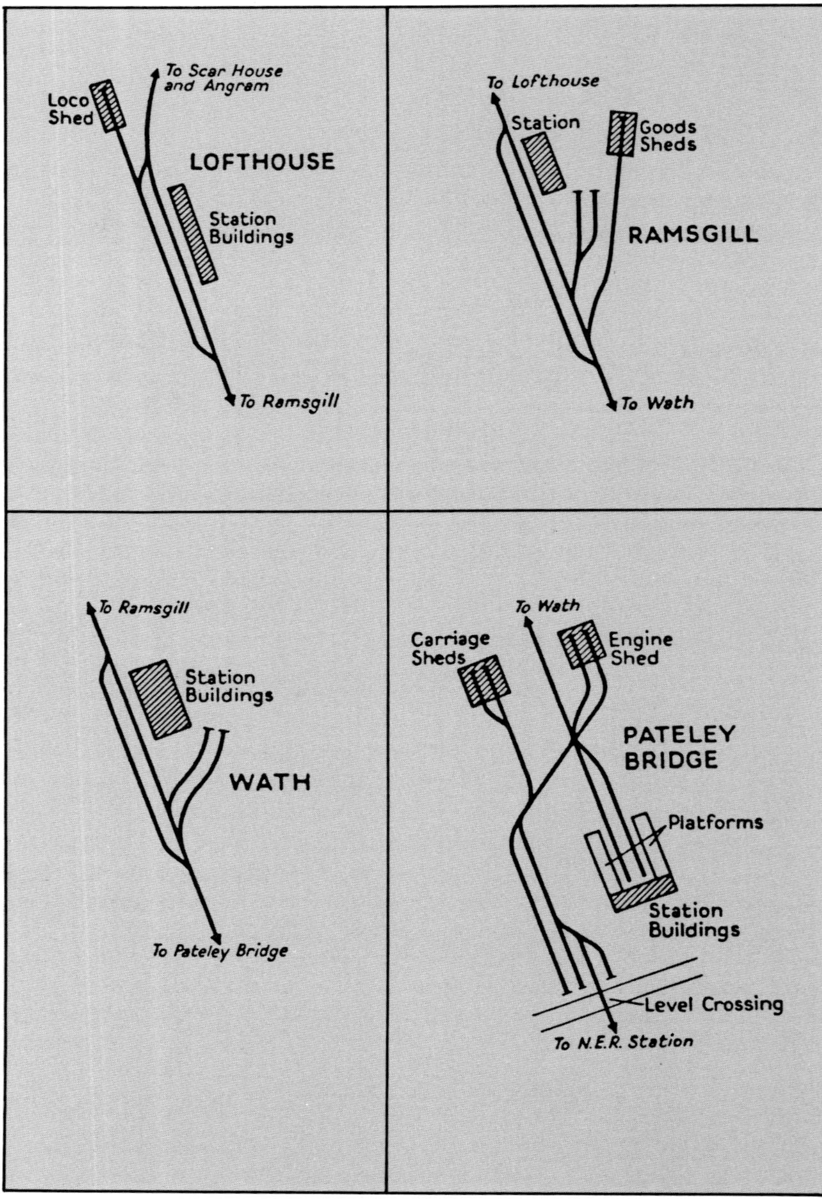

Schematic trackplans of the four Nidd Valley Light Railway stations.

original Gouthwaite Hall was an Elizabethan manor house built by the Yorke family on the site of an earlier house dating back to Norman times.

Very soon, the train begins to reduce speed, and we approach Ramsgill station, which we have reached in fifteen minutes from Pateley Bridge. This station would be more appropriately named 'Bouthwaite', for it is situated almost a third of a mile from Ramsgill. Quite close to the station is Bouthwaite Grange, which was one of the properties belonging to the monks of Fountains Abbey, and is known to have been in existence in 1539.

Ramsgill to Lofthouse

The station itself is similar to that at Wath, except that there are three short sidings, plus an additional longer siding which was used to accommodate surplus stock at one time.

The village of Ramsgill is famous in being the birthplace of Eugene Aram (1704–1759), who later taught as tutor at Gouthwaite Hall. In later life, he became a murderer, having killed a man near Knaresborough, for which he was hanged at York in 1759.

As the train leaves Ramsgill on the last stage of its journey to Lofthouse, it is soon apparent that the valley is narrowing. For about a mile, the railway runs some distance from the River Nidd which winds its way along the valley to our left. At Low Sikes, the railway crosses the main road on the level, before heading off through the fields for the last three-quarters of a mile or so to Lofthouse. Soon we are drawing into Lofthouse Station, and it is journey's end for the other travellers, but we are fortunate in being able to travel over the contractor's line to the very head of the valley.

Lofthouse to Scar

Although Lofthouse is the terminus of the Nidd Valley Light Railway, its appearance does not give that impression. This is because the through line to Scar House makes it seem more like an intermediate station than a terminus. There are a couple of sidings, plus a small goods shed which was originally built to house the special Committee coach. The rest of the passengers from our train have by now left the platform, and the train is slowly backed clear of the platform to await the arrival of our connecting train from Scar House. Soon, a plume of smoke heralds the arrival of our train, which consists of three carriages hauled by 0–6–0ST *Watson*, looking extremely clean and smart.

A couple of dozen people alight from the incoming train, presumably on their way to Pateley Bridge, or perhaps Harrogate. We board the train, and it is immediately obvious that these carriages are used for the transport of workers and their families, for the condition is not as good as the stock we have just left on the Nidd Valley Light Railway. It is difficult to realise that there are two separate railway systems serving the valley, yet sharing common track and stations. Suddenly, the sound of another locomotive is heard, and this joins the head of our train, leaving *Watson* at the rear to act as banker for the journey up to Scar House. We have just time to leap out of our carriage to take a quick look at the new arrival, which is another 0–6–0ST named *Blythe*.

With a shrill blast on the whistle, our short train pulls out of Lofthouse for its six mile trip to Scar House, over what must be one of the most spectacular branch lines in the north of England. Shortly after leaving the station, the track turns through almost sixty degrees to the right, and soon enters the private section of track which has a metalled road running alongside it all the way to the reservoir site. The train soon begins to climb, and with long stretches at a gradient of 1 in 40, it is not surprising that our journey will take around 40 minutes. There are also many sharp curves to be negotiated *en route*. As the gradient increases, it can be appreciated why it is not uncommon to have heavy goods trains double-headed on this stretch of line, with two more locomotives at the rear to act as bankers.

The line runs along a shelf cut out of the hill-side in places, and far below in the narrow valley lies the River Nidd. Way above us on the opposite side of the valley are a few tiny farmsteads for whose occupants the sight of the train must be a welcome break in the monotonous isolation.

About half-way on our journey we encounter the only tunnel on the Nidd Valley Light Railway. Here, close to Goyden Pot, a 180 yard tunnel was constructed in the early 1920s in order to ease the very sharp curve used hitherto. The old line was retained and re-laid, and now forms a 500 yard long loop, to enable trains to pass at busy periods.

Soon the gradient begins to ease, and we are approaching the end of our journey. At Woodale, another loop line is passed, and then we begin to slow down for the approach to Scar House, a thousand feet above sea level.

Scar House and Angram

The one thing that impresses most when leaving the train at Scar House is the enormity of the site. That such a hive of activity should exist in such an isolated spot as this is almost too much for the eye to take in immediately. The sounds of the site are not in keeping with the moorland surroundings. No curlew or grouse are heard here, but instead the sound of steam hammers, giant cranes, locomotive whistles, and the voices of countless workmen, many only just visible in the distant parts of the site. The sight and sound of distant locomotives leads us to the foreman's office to enquire if it will be possible to look more closely at the railway. A brief chat to the foreman about the railway ensures us a special pass giving us the freedom of the site on condition that we do not endanger ourselves or hinder the workmen.

The easiest way to explore the railway is to follow the tracks around the site. Close to the housing area, but at a lower level is the engine shed. Here we find *Beatty,* a Manning Wardle 0–6–0ST of 1905 resting from its duties around the site. Following another track, we descend closer to the dam, and are fortunate to be able to cross to the north side where there is more railway activity. *Allenby,* another Manning Wardle 0–6–0ST appears with a short train of archaic side-tipping wagons, as we begin the ascent of the hillside towards the quarry. Once there, we have a spectacular view of the site, and to the west we can clearly see Angram Reservoir where work ended some twelve years ago. It is in this elevated location that we may find the three 0–4–0ST's which are normally only to be found at work here. In the stone yard is the first of these, *Craven,* with a short train of wagons being loaded with huge stone blocks by a powerful crane alongside.

From the stone yard, a double track inclined tramway leads up to the quarry where the stone for the dam is obtained. The quarry is over 500 feet above the dam, and is something of a surprise to find another 0–4–0ST, *Trotter* hard at work. Presumably it had reached its work place by means of the inclined tramway, which must have caused a few tense moments as it was winched upwards.

Returning to ground level from the quarry, we continue beyond the main construction site, and here the tracks end, but there are still signs of the track-bed of the former line to Angram. Angram is about 1½ miles further along the valley, and we have time to follow the traces westwards to see what remains of the railway and village can still be found. The end of the line is something of a disappointment, for no trace remains of the village which once housed 500 men, for much of it was moved downstream to Scar House when construction began there. There are indications that several sidings once existed at Angram, but beyond that, little else can be identified.

And so we make our way back to Scar House; our return train is already waiting at the temporary wooden platform, and soon we are on our way back down the valley to civilisation, and the Nidd Valley Light Railway which will return us to Pateley Bridge, and then home via the North Eastern Railway.

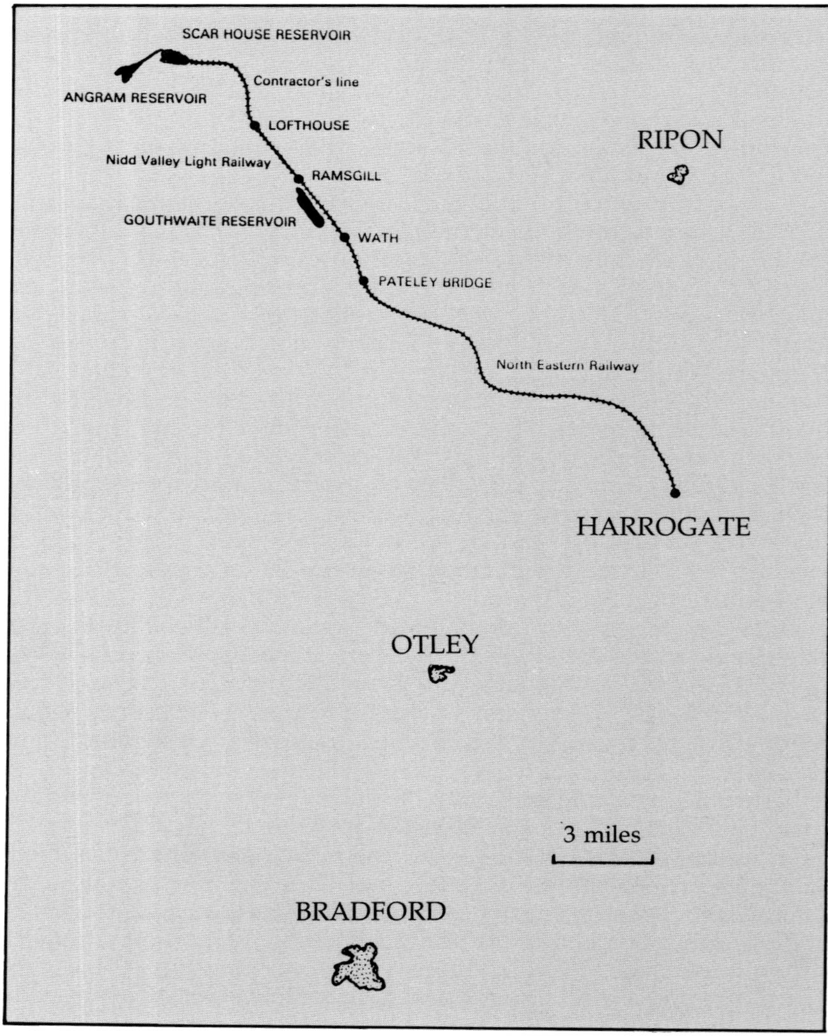

Map showing the Nidd Valley Light Railway in relation to Bradford.

Chapter Seven

Locomotives and Rolling Stock

The Nidd Valley Light Railway used five steam locomotives and one steam railcar on its passenger services between Pateley Bridge and Lofthouse during its 22 year existence. Until now, the entire rolling stock used on the line has been attributed to the Nidd Valley Light Railway, but close examination of the minutes of the Bradford Corporation Waterworks Committee reveals no mention of the remaining locomotives, so it must be assumed that the other locomotives and some of the carriages were owned by John Best & Sons Ltd, the contractor on both the Angram and Scar House reservoir construction sites. This is borne out by references in the early correspondence of the railway to "Best's engine", and also by the fact that the financial records of the railway contain references to the purchase of only 5 steam locomotives and the steam railcar.

Consequently, details of the rolling stock used on the line between Pateley Bridge, Lofthouse, Scar House and Angram are divided into two distinct sections, representing those owned by the Nidd Valley Light Railway proper, (i.e. Bradford Corporation), and those owned by John Best & Sons Ltd, the contractor.

NIDD VALLEY LIGHT RAILWAY

Locomotives

No. 1 *Holdsworth*. Beyer, Peacock 4–4–0T (Works No. 707), built 1866 for the Metropolitan Railway, No. 20. Weight 45 tons. Overall length 33ft 1in. Boiler pressure 130 lb. per sq. inch. Cylinders 17¼in. × 24in. Driving wheels 5ft 10in. Coal capacity 1 ton. Water capacity 1000 gallons. Tractive effort 12,680 lb. On acquisition by the NVLR, the condensing apparatus was removed, and a cab was fitted by the Metropolitan at their Neasden Works. Named after Alderman W. Holdsworth, the Chairman of the railway. This locomotive was advertised for sale in the *Yorkshire Post* newspaper on 30th November, 1912, but it would seem that there were no takers, for it was scrapped at Scar House around 1920.

No. 2 *Milner*. Beyer, Peacock 4–4–0T (Works No. 1878). Built 1879 for the Metropolitan Railway, No. 34. Weight 46¾ tons. Overall length 31ft 10in. Boiler pressure 160lb. per sq. inch. Cylinders 17¼in. × 24in. Driving wheels 5ft 10in. Coal capacity 1½ tons. Water capacity 1140 gallons. Tractive effort 13,056 lb. On acquisition by the NVLR, the condensing apparatus was removed, and a cab was fitted by the Metropolitan at their Neasden Works. Named after Alderman D. Milner, the Vice-Chairman of the railway. Withdrawn from service in

1909, it was presumably unused until December 1913, when it was purchased by Brooke's of Lightcliffe, near Halifax. It was then leased to one of their subsidiaries, the North Wales Granite Company Ltd, for work at one of their quarries, and was subsequently re-named *Conway*. It was certainly used in North Wales until the end of 1918, by 1926 it was in store at Lightcliffe. However, it was back in North Wales, at a quarry near Penmaenmawr by the summer of 1929. In 1930, it was sold to T.W. Ward for scrap, and fetched £70.

Milner (II). Hudswell, Clarke 0–6–0T (Works No. 882). Built 1909. Weight 29 tons. Boiler pressure 160lb. per sq. inch. Outside cylinders 12in. × 18in. Driving wheels 3ft 3½in. This locomotive was purchased new at a cost of £1,300 to replace the original No. 2 *Milner*. It proved to be an exceptionally sturdy locomotive, and handled the majority of passenger workings. It was fitted with a small, high-speed reciprocating engine and dynamo for train-lighting, which were supplied by Messrs Harper, Phillips & Co. Ltd, of Grimsby. It was withdrawn in 1936, and was sold at the auction in June 1937 for £650 to Sir Lindsay Parkinson, the contractor. It was later sold to Caffin & Co., and was last recorded with George Wimpey at an open-cast coal mine near Cardiff in 1956.

Gadie (I). Hudswell, Clarke & Co. Ltd 0–4–0ST (Works No. 1411). Built 1920. Boiler pressure 140lb. per sq. inch. Outside cylinders 14in. × 20in. Driving wheels 3ft 7in. Used mainly for working on the dam at Scar House, and around the reservoir and quarry. Named after Anthony Gadie, Lord Mayor of Bradford, 1920–1921, who cut the first sod at Scar House on 5th October, 1921, and later laid the first concrete on the site. In 1925, when Andrew Barclay 0–6–0ST No. 1866 was delivered, *Gadie* (I) was re-named *Craven* after Alderman P.L. Craven, Deputy Chairman of the Waterworks Committee, 1922–1925. *Craven* was sold to the Bradford Corporation Gas Department for £700 in June 1929.

Gadie (II). Andrew Barclay Sons & Co. Ltd. 0–6–0ST (Works No. 1866). Built 1925. Boiler pressure 160lb. per sq. inch. Outside cylinders 14in. × 22in. Driving wheels 3ft 5in. Used for working through trains of coal, cement and other materials from Pateley Bridge. Purchased new by the Nidd Valley Light Railway. At some time after purchase it was fitted with an electric lighting generator supplied by Harper, Phillips & Co. Ltd of Grimsby. Sold in June 1937 for £1,030 to a Scottish foundry.

Hill. Kerr, Stuart & Co. Ltd steam railcar (Works No. 906). Built 1905 for the Great Western Railway, No. 15. Bodywork by Hurst, Nelson & Co. Ltd, with seating for 48 passengers, plus luggage space. Length

60ft. Boiler pressure 160lb. per sq. inch. Cylinders 9in. × 15in. Driving wheels 3ft 3in. The mechanical portion was arranged so that it could be driven from either end. Sold in May 1920 to J.F. Wake of Darlington, but re-sold to Bradford Corporation with whom it entered service in July 1920. Named after the Lord Mayor of Bradford for 1908–1909, Sir James Hill. Withdrawn when passenger services ceased on 31st December, 1929. Sold for scrap in June 1937. Part of the body was found thirty years later in a Leeds scrapyard, still bearing its original GWR fittings and notices. Subsequent fate unknown, but presumed scrapped.

It is also believed that a Honeywill 40 hp petrol tractor was owned by the Nidd Valley Light Railway. This was acquired in September 1923 for £350, though its life was fairly short at Scar House, as it was found to be too wide and too heavy, and was subsequently transferred to the Chellow Heights Waterworks in Bradford, where it is understood to have remained until about 1952.

Carriage stock

Few details have survived of the carriage stock used on the Nidd Valley Light Railway, and it is not known what numbering scheme was used, if any.

The original intention had been to purchase new carriages, and tenders were invited for the supply of two first class and two third class composite coaches, plus three third class saloons. In the event, none were ordered, and it was eventually decided to purchase ten four-wheeled carriages from the Metropolitan Railway at a cost of £80 each, and these arrived early in 1906, well before the line was completed. Some had four first class compartments, whilst the remainder had five third class compartments. It is believed that all had been built by Cravens around 1887, but their former Metropolitan numbers are not known. All but two of these carriages were withdrawn by 1927, but details of their fate are not known.

Two other items of carriage stock were owned by the Nidd Valley Light Railway, these being used by members of the Waterworks Committee and by important visitors.

The first was a four-wheeled single deck tramcar saloon, ordered from Hurst, Nelson & Company in February 1904. This car was similar to a double deck electric tramcar which Hurst, Nelson had exhibited at the 1902 Tramways Exhibition, and which later passed to Ayr Corporation Tramways. An unusual feature of both these cars were the stained glass panels which separated the main saloon windows. The Nidd Valley saloon was delivered in March 1906, and was elaborately lined out, and carried the Corporation coat of arms on the centre of the side panels. It is believed that the car seated 20 passengers. The car was apparently used by civic parties visiting the construction sites, and again on the opening day of the railway, 11th September, 1907, though it seems to have been little used after this date. Around 1910, it was returned to Hurst, Nelson who used the underframe for another item of rolling stock, and the body remained at the Motherwell yard until 1912 when it was acquired by the Wantage Tramway. It was then re-fitted and became Wantage No. 5, though photographic evidence of its use on this line has not survived.

The second saloon was apparently delivered during the 1920s, and was a four-wheeled coach, believed to have been built by Pickerings. The body had four windows per side, and an open observation platform at one end. It was lettered 'Bradford Corporation Nidd Railway'.

Goods Stock

Very little in the way of goods stock was owned by the Nidd Valley Light Railway. The majority of goods trains to the reservoir sites originated on the North Eastern Railway, and consisted of their wagons. The following NVLR goods wagons were owned:

Brake vans 1–2:	Four-wheeled brake vans built by Hurst, Nelson & Co. Ltd at a cost of £141 each.
Open goods wagons:	Six four-wheeled goods wagons were purchased from Hurst, Nelson at a total cost of £373 10*s* 0*d*. It is not known what numbers these carried.

Liveries

The livery adopted for the original locomotives was the Metropolitan Railway's colour scheme of red with yellow lining. When the two Nidd Valley locomotives were repainted at Neasden, however, they were given a darker yellow lining to that which they had previously carried. The Bradford Corporation coat of arms adorned the centre of the side panels, and was surmounted by the engine name. The words 'Bradford Corporation' were also carried, the wording being split either side of the coat of arms. Brass number plates were also mounted on the bunker.

When *Milner* (II) was delivered in 1909, it carried an overall black livery with polished black dome and copper-topped chimney. No signs of Corporation ownership were carried on this locomotive, and the numbering scheme which had commenced with the ex-Metropolitan locomotives was discontinued.

Holdsworth on shed. *Pearce Higgins Collection, National Railway Museum, York*

The opening day, 11th September, 1907. Locomotive *Holdsworth* and the official party photographed at Gouthwaite Lodge.

Courtesy Yorkshire Water Authority

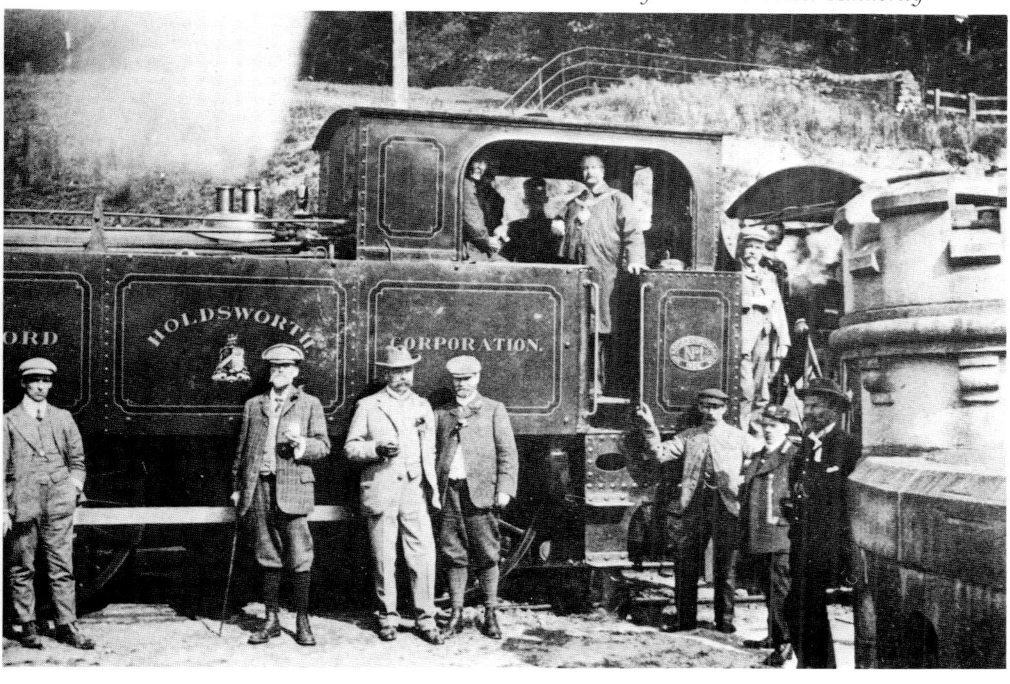

Scar House, October 1921, on the occasion of the cutting of the first sod of the reservoir. The "Bradford Corporation Private Car" is at the end of the train.
Courtesy Yorkshire Water Authority

The first locomotive *Gadie* seen at Scar House on 17th June, 1924, on the occasion of the laying of the first consignment of concrete at the Scar House Dam. *Courtesy Yorkshire Water Authority*

The second locomotive to be named *Gadie*, photographed when new in 1925 at Pateley Bridge. *Photomatic Ltd*

Another view of the second *Gadie* at Lofthouse in 1928. *Photomatic Ltd*

Avonside Engine Company 0–6–0ST *Blythe* at Pateley Bridge. *Photomatic Ltd*

Originally named *Mitchell,* this Hudswell, Clarke 0–6–0ST was renamed *Illingworth* around 1930. *Courtesy Yorkshire Water Authority*

Ian Hamilton — the oldest locomotive used by the contractors. Built by Hudswell, Clarke in 1897. *Photomatic Ltd*

Watson simmers in the sun at Lofthouse. *Photomatic Ltd*

Trotter rests in the quarry at Scar House. *Photomatic Ltd*

Haig towards the end of its days.
Pearce Higgins Collection, National Railway Museum, York

A rake of contractor's carriages after their sale to Sheffield Corporation's Ladybower Reservoir Railway. *Lens of Sutton*

The Nidd Valley Light Railway steam railcar at the end of its days. *Neville Stead Collection*

Close-up view of the archaic tipping wagons used on the reservoir construction work. *Courtesy Yorkshire Water Authority*

With *Gadie* leading, a double-headed train of tipper wagons sets out to the construction site at Scar House. *Courtesy Yorkshire Water Authority*

The steam railcar was painted in a maroon livery, and carried the lettering 'Nidd Valley Light Railway' and 'Bradford Corporation' in addition to the Corporation coat of arms.

Carriage stock was painted maroon, with the words 'Bradford Corporation'. It is not known what livery the two saloon coaches carried.

Goods brake vans 1–2 were grey, whilst the open goods wagons were a dark bluish grey, with 'BC' in large white letters.

JOHN BEST & SONS LTD

Locomotives

The number of steam locomotives employed by John Best & Sons Ltd on the Angram and Scar House Reservoir contracts is not known for certain. One source suggests as many as 15 were at work in 1925, though only 10 can be positively identified, whilst two others are known to have existed, though details are sparse. The figure of 15 could be correct, for it is understood that 8 were acquired in 1925 when the work on Scar House reservoir was at its height. It seems evident that some locomotives served only for short periods of time, presumably moving to other construction sites. The following locomotives are positively known to have been employed by Best's in Upper Nidderdale:

Allenby. Manning, Wardle 0–6–0ST (Works No. 1379). Built 1898. Boiler pressure 125 lb. per sq. inch. Inside cylinders 13in. × 18in. Driving wheels 3ft. New to Price & Wills, contractor, of Battle, Sussex, where it was named *Sidley*. To Topham Jones & Railton, contractors in 1907. Acquired by Best's – date unknown. It was presumably named after Field Marshall Allenby, who had served in the Zulu and Boer wars, and was the British cavalry leader at Mons in 1914. It was used mainly for working on the dam at Scar House, and around the reservoir and quarry. After use by Best's, it was acquired by Sir Lindsay Parkinson, with whom it retained its name *Allenby*, and gained the number 206. The National Coal Board became its next owner, who used it at Dalton Screens, near Wakefield. It returned to Sir Lindsay Parkinson by 1950, with whom it was last recorded.

Beatty. Manning, Wardle 0–6–0ST (Works No. 1669). Built 1905. Boiler pressure 125 lb. per sq. inch. Inside cylinders 13in. × 18in. Driving wheels 3ft. New to Easton Gibbs & Son Ltd, contractors of Dunston-on-Tyne, with whom it was numbered 59. Acquired by Best's – date unknown. Named after Earl Beatty, Commander of the Battle Cruiser Squadron, 1912–1916. Used mainly for working on the dam at Scar House, and around the reservoir and quarry. Sold to Raine & Co. Ltd, Delta Iron & Steel Works, Swalwell, County Durham. Withdrawn in 1957, and scrapped in 1959.

Blythe. Avonside Engine Co. 0–6–0ST (Works No. 1894). Built 1922. Boiler pressure 160 lb. per sq. inch. Outside cylinders 14½in. × 20in. Driving wheels 3ft 3in. Used for working through trains of coal, cement and other materials from Pateley Bridge. Fitted with electric lighting generator supplied by Harper, Phillips & Co. Ltd of Grimsby. Named after Thomas Blythe, the Lord Mayor of Bradford, 1921–1922.

Haig. Manning, Wardle 0–6–0ST (Works No. 1224). Built 1890. Boiler pressure 125 lb. per sq. inch. Inside cylinders 13in. × 20in. Driving wheels 3ft 3in. New to Logan & Hemingway, contractors, at Gretna, with whom it was named *Pioneer*. On acquisition by Best's, it was re-named *Haig* after Field Marshall Earl Haig of Bemersyde who had been given the freedom of the City of Bradford in 1921. Nothing is known of this locomotive after sale.

Ian Hamilton. Hudswell, Clarke & Co. Ltd 0–6–0ST (Works No. 480). Built 1897. Boiler pressure 150 lb. per sq. inch. Outside cylinders 13in. × 18in. Driving wheels 3ft 0½in. Delivered new to Trent Ironworks, Frodingham, Lincolnshire, and named *Trent No. 4*. Presumably re-named after the British General, Sir Ian Standish Hamilton.

Kitchener. Peckett & Sons Ltd 0–6–0ST (Works No. 939). Built 1902. Boiler pressure 140 lb. per sq. inch. Outside cylinders 14in. × 20in. Driving wheels 3ft 6in. Presumably named after Lord Kitchener who was British Commander-in-Chief during the Boer War which ended in the year the engine was built. Sold at the auction in 1937 for around £700.

Mitchell. Hudswell, Clarke & Co. Ltd 0–6–0ST (Works No. 1208). Built 1916. Boiler pressure 160 lb. per sq. inch. Outside cylinders 14in. × 20in. Driving wheels 3ft 7in. Delivered new to the Ministry of Munitions at Gretna, and named *Mitchell*. Date of acquisition by Best's unknown, but it did not need re-naming as the railway already had a personality named 'Mitchell' connected with it. This was Lewis Mitchell, the Bradford Corporation Waterworks Engineer who was appointed Engineer and Manager of the Nidd Valley Light Railway in January 1920. Mitchell resigned from his post in October 1930, and the locomotive was re-named *Illingworth* after Alderman W. Illingworth, the Deputy Chairman of the Waterworks Committee, 1926–1940 and 1941–1945.

Stringer. Andrew Barclay Sons & Co. Ltd 0–6–0ST (Works No. 1877). Built 1925. Boiler pressure 160 lb. per sq. inch. Outside cylinders 10in. × 18in. Driving wheels 3ft. Named after Joseph Stringer, the Lord Mayor of Bradford, 1925–1926.

Trotter. Andrew Barclay Sons & Co. Ltd 0–4–0ST (Works No. 1810). Built 1925. Boiler pressure 160 lb. per sq. inch. Outside cylinders 10in. × 18in. Driving wheels 3ft. Named after Herbert M. Trotter, the Lord Mayor of Bradford, 1923–1924.

Watson. Hudswell, Clarke & Co. Ltd 0–6–0ST (Works No. 1197). Built 1916. Boiler pressure 160 lb. per sq. inch. Outside cylinders 14in. × 20in. Driving wheels 3ft 7in. Delivered new to the Ministry of Munitions at Gretna, and carried the name 'D.E.S.', being one of two locomotives to carry this abbreviation. Date of acquisition by Best's is unknown, but re-named *Watson*, after James Watson, a locomotive superintendent on the Nidd Valley Light Railway. Later sold for use at Sheffield Corporation's Ladybower Reservoir scheme. Sold again in June 1948 to the National Coal Board for use at Woolley Colliery, near Barnsley. Disposed of by 1969.

It is known that two additional locomotives were owned by Best's and worked in Nidderdale, though exact details are not known, though photographic evidence exists of both.

The first is depicted on a photograph on display in the Nidderdale Museum at Pateley Bridge, and was an 0–4–0ST, possibly built by Barclay. It is known to have been used by Best's during the construction of Angram Reservoir sometime between 1906 and 1919, and is regularly referred to in Bradford Corporation Waterworks Department correspondence as "Best's Engine".

The second was an 0–6–0ST, possibly built by Manning, Wardle. All that is known is that it was sold to Leeds Corporation around 1921 for use on the construction of the Middleton housing estate. It was used from 1921 to 1924 on works trains from Hunslet Carr to Middleton Park Road, and on completion of the work was sold to an owner in Manchester. It is believed that a driver from Best's contract accompanied the locomotive from Nidderdale to Leeds, where he worked with his engine, and also moved with it to Manchester.

Carriage Stock

Nothing is known of the early carriage stock used by Best's, indeed it may be that workers' trains were composed of Nidd Valley Light Railway stock. In the mid-1920s, twelve four-wheeled carriages were obtained from the Maryport & Carlisle Railway. Photographic evidence suggests that these were of two different types, some being four-compartment vehicles, whilst others had five compartments. Six of these carriages were later sold to Richard Baillis for use on workmen's trains from Bamford to the Ladybower Reservoir site which Sheffield Corporation was constructing, and it is believed that they were hauled to their new home by locomotive *Watson* which was sold to the same concern. Two of those sold were four compartment vehicles, whilst the remainder had five compartments. Some sources suggest that the coaches were never in fact used at Ladybower, and were used instead as site-huts. If they were used on workmen's trains, they survived until 1943, but no further trace of them is known.

Goods Stock

A number of archaic wooden-bodied side-tipping wagons were used around the reservoir sites, but little else is known of rolling stock used by Best's. One source suggests that a number of wagons were purchased second-hand from the London, Midland & Scottish and London & North Eastern Railways, but there appears to be no written evidence to support this statement.

Liveries

Nothing is known of the locomotive liveries used by Best's – they are presumed to have been black. Carriage and wagon liveries are unknown.

Several of the locomotives which bore 'local connection' names, such as *Stringer*, *Trotter* and *Watson* are believed to have had nameplates specially cast by Isaac Walker & Son, of Shipley Brass Works, Windhill, near Shipley, and it may be that the Corporation paid for these plates.

BRADFORD CORPORATION
Nidd Valley Light Railway.
Third Class.
LOFTHOUSE
TO
PATELEY BRIDGE
FARE 4½D.
Issued subject to time tables and to Corporation's rules and regulations in force relating to the said railway.
577
Police & Military.

Ticket by courtesy of Premier Tickets, Leicester

Chapter Eight

Fares, Tickets & Timetables

Fares

For the opening of the railway in 1907, the following fares were established:

Adult Singles (1st/3rd class)

PATELEY BRIDGE			
3d/1½*d*	WATH		
8d/*4d*	*5d*/2½*d*	RAMSGILL	
1*s*/*6d*	*9d*/4½*d*	*4d*/*2d*	LOFTHOUSE

Adult Returns (1st/3rd class)

PATELEY BRIDGE			
6d/*3d*	WATH		
1*s* *4d*/*8d*	10*d*/*5d*	RAMSGILL	
2*s*/1*s*	1*s* *6d*/*9d*	*8d*/*4d*	LOFTHOUSE

Child Singles (1st/3rd class)

PATELEY BRIDGE			
2d/1*d*	WATH		
4d/*2d*	*3d*/1½*d*	RAMSGILL	
6d/*3d*	*5d*/2½*d*	*2d*/1*d*	LOFTHOUSE

Child Returns (1st/3rd class)

PATELEY BRIDGE			
3d/1½*d*	WATH		
8d/*4d*	*5d*/2½*d*	RAMSGILL	
1*s*/*6d*	*9d*/4½*d*	*4d*/*2d*	LOFTHOUSE

Other fares included:

Dogs – Single to any station	*3d*
– Return to any station	*5d*
Cycle or Mailcart – single to any station	*6d*
– return to any station	1*s*
Police or Military	
Pateley Bridge – Lofthouse return	*9d*

Return Excursion Fares (1st/3rd class)

Pateley Bridge – Wath	*6d*/*3d*
Pateley Bridge – Ramsgill	1*s*/*6d*
Pateley Bridge – Lofthouse	1*s* *6d*/*9d*

Despite the apparent closure of Wath and Ramsgill stations late in 1921, it was still possible to book tickets to and from these stations, with the exception that only single fares were available between the two.

At its meeting on 12th April, 1929, the Waterworks Committee discussed the reduction of fares to compete with the Pateley Bridge to Lofthouse bus service. By this time, the adult fares were as follows: (Single/Return)

PATELEY BRIDGE			
2½*d*/5*d*	WATH		
6*d*/1*s*	4*d*/–	RAMSGILL	
9*d*/1*s* 6*d*	7*d*/1*s* 2*d*	?/?	LOFTHOUSE

The following reduced fares were suggested: (Single/Return)

PATELEY BRIDGE			
1½*d*/3*d*	WATH		
4*d*/8*d*	3*d*/–	RAMSGILL	
6*d*/1*s*	5*d*/10*d*	?/?	LOFTHOUSE

It was also decided to offer a 9*d* return fare between Pateley Bridge and Lofthouse on Thursdays and Saturdays only. A decision was deferred at the April meeting, but the reductions came into force on 2nd July, 1929, though they were too late to save the railway.

From the beginning of operations, contract tickets were available as indicated on *Plate A*.

Tickets

Edmondson type card tickets were issued for all fares, these being headed 'BRADFORD CORPORATION Nidd Valley Light Railway'. The different types were categorised by colour, as follows:

Adult singles	– 1st Class	– White
	– 3rd Class	– Blue
Adult Returns	– 1st Class	– Yellow
	– 3rd Class	– Orange
Child Singles	– 1st Class	– White with red CHILD overprint
	– 3rd Class	– Blue with red CHILD overprint
Child Returns	– 1st Class	– Yellow with Red CHILD overprint
	– 3rd Class	– Orange with red CHILD overprint

City of Bradford.

NIDD VALLEY LIGHT RAILWAY.

CONTRACT TICKETS

Are issued between any of the Stations on this Light Railway at the rates shewn below, and can be obtained through the Secretary of the said Light Railway by giving 7 days' Notice on a written application.

STATIONS.	Miles.	12 MONTHS.		6 MONTHS.		3 MONTHS.	
		1st Class.	3rd Class.	1st Class.	3rd Class.	1st Class.	3rd Class.
		£ s. d.	£ s. d.	£ s. d.	£ s. d.	£ s. d.	£ s. d.
Pateley Bridge to Wath ...	1½	3 10 0	2 0 0	1 18 6	1 2 0	1 1 0	0 12 0
,, Ramsgill ...	4	6 6 0	4 0 0	3 9 6	2 4 0	1 18 0	1 4 0
,, Lofthouse...	6	6 16 6	5 0 0	3 15 6	2 15 0	2 1 6	1 10 0
Wath to Pateley Bridge ...	1½	3 10 0	2 0 0	1 18 6	1 2 0	1 1 0	0 12 0
,, Ramsgill ...	2½	5 0 0	2 15 0	2 15 0	1 10 3	1 10 0	0 16 6
,, Lofthouse ...	4½	6 8 9	4 5 0	3 11 0	2 6 9	1 19 0	1 5 6
Ramsgill to Pateley Bridge.	4	6 6 0	4 0 0	3 9 6	2 4 0	1 18 0	1 4 0
,, Wath ...	2½	5 0 0	2 15 0	2 15 0	1 10 3	1 10 0	0 16 6
,, Lofthouse ...	2	4 10 0	2 10 0	2 9 6	1 7 6	1 7 0	0 15 0
Lofthouse to Pateley Bridge.	6	6 16 6	5 0 0	3 15 6	2 15 0	2 1 6	1 10 0
,, Ramsgill ...	2	4 10 0	2 10 0	2 9 6	1 7 6	1 7 0	0 15 0
,, Wath ...	4½	6 8 9	4 5 0	3 11 0	2 6 9	1 19 0	1 5 6

Contract tickets are issued at half-rate to *children under 18 years of age* if a certificate of age is given on the application form.

All Contract Tickets issued by the Corporation are subject to the notices, regulations, and conditions contained in the current Time Tables and Time Bills of the Corporation, and to the following further conditions:—

The Corporation shall not be liable for any alteration in or discontinuance of any advertised train without notice, nor for stoppage of or delay to any train from whatever cause arising.

The holder must show his ticket to any officer of the Corporation when required so to do, and in default will be charged the ordinary fare for the journey travelled.

A Contract Ticket must be given up immediately on expiration, and any attempt to use it after the date of expiry, or to use it irregularly, renders the holder liable to the same penalties and obligations as a passenger travelling without a ticket.

A Contract Ticket is not transferable, and if it is used by any other person than the person to whom it is issued, or is used irregularly, it will be forfeited, and the holder will render himself liable to be proceeded against under the Regulation of Railways Act, 1889.

The Corporation reserve to themselves the right to decline to issue or renew any Contract Ticket.

BY ORDER,

WM. THOS. CROFT,

SECRETARY.

TOWN HALL, BRADFORD,
October, 1907.

Plate A

Other tickets were as follows:

Dogs Single for any station – fawn with horizontal green band
Return for any station – white with horizontal green band
Police and Military – orange returns with horizontal red band
Cycles and Mailcarts – Single for any station – green with horizontal purple band
– Return for any station – colour not known

Excursion tickets

Excursion tickets were issued from either Pateley Bridge or Lofthouse, and these broke the established colour-coded sequence by having yellow tickets issued at Pateley Bridge, and orange ones at Lofthouse. In both cases, the children's tickets were the same colour as the adult ones, with the exception of a horizontal red band. These tickets enabled the holder to break his journey at either or both of the intermediate stations, and to continue by a later train.

It is also known that some tickets existed in a tri-colour effect, with pink, white and blue vertical bands, though it is not known what use was made of these. It is possible that they were introduced to meet the reduced fares introduced in July 1929. In all cases, the tickets were printed by M. Harland & Sons Ltd.

Timetables

Although the Nidd Valley Light Railway produced timetable leaflets, none seem to have survived, and so we are forced to find details of the train services from other sources such as Bradshaw.

To commence operations, four return trains were planned for each day except Sundays, when no trains ran. This schedule remained fairly rigid for several years. The following was the 1910 timetable:

				A	
	am	am	pm	pm	pm
Pateley Bridge	8.40	10.20	1.30	4.10	6.00
Wath	8.45	10.25	1.35	4.15	6.05
Ramsgill	8.55	10.35	1.45	4.25	6.15
Lofthouse	9.00	10.40	1.50	4.30	6.20
				A	
Lofthouse	9.15	11.05	2.55	4.50	6.30
Ramsgill	9.20	11.10	3.00	4.55	6.35
Wath	9.30	11.20	3.10	5.05	6.45
Pateley Bridge	9.35	11.25	3.15	5.10	6.50

The services marked 'A' above ran only on Wednesdays and Saturdays, which were then the half-day closing and market days respectively. The winter service was identical to the above, with the exception that the 6.00 pm departure from Pateley Bridge, and the 6.30 pm return journey were withdrawn.

During World War I, it was found necessary to reduce the service to three trains per day. We are fortunate in having more detailed notes on the following timetable, which was introduced on 1st November, 1918:

	am	am	pm
Pateley Bridge	8.30	10.30	3.45
Wath	8.35	10.35	3.50
Ramsgill	8.48	10.48	4.03
Lofthouse	8.55	10.55	4.10
		noon	
Lofthouse	9.15	12.00	4.20
Ramsgill	9.20	12.05	4.25
Wath	9.30	12.15	4.35
Pateley Bridge	9.35	12.20	4.40

No trains were operated on Sundays. Special services were to be operated on Bank Holidays as follows:

Christmas Eve: an additional train was to be operated, departing from Pateley Bridge at 5.00 pm and calling as required at intermediate stations to Lofthouse, returning from there at 5.30 pm.
Christmas Day: No service.
Boxing Day: Normal service.
Good Friday: No service.
Easter Saturday and Easter Monday: an additional train to be operated, departing from Pateley Bridge at 5.00 pm, and calling at intermediate stations as required to Lofthouse, returning to Pateley Bridge at 5.30 pm.

By 1922, when traffic was greater, a further return trip was added to the pre-war timetable, with slight alterations to timings compared with the 1915 timetable, as shown below:

	am	am	pm	pm	pm
Pateley Bridge	8.30	10.20	1.30	3.30	5.00
Wath	8.35	10.25	1.35	3.35	5.05
Ramsgill	8.47	10.37	1.47	3.47	5.17
Lofthouse	8.53	10.43	1.53	3.53	5.23
Lofthouse	9.10	11.00	2.00	4.10	5.30
Ramsgill	9.16	11.06	2.06	4.16	5.36
Wath	9.25	11.15	2.15	4.25	5.45
Pateley Bridge	9.30	11.20	2.20	4.30	5.50

Throughout the existence of the Nidd Valley Light Railway numerous workmen's trains were operated for the benefit of those engaged on the reservoir construction sites. These were operated by the contractor's locomotives, and timetables varied from time to time. In addition, some trains are known to have been run only as far as Lofthouse, as this 1927 timetable shows:

	Tuesdays	Thursdays	Saturdays
	am	am	pm
Scar Village dep.	8.30	8.30	1.40
Lofthouse arr.	9.30	9.30	2.20
	pm	pm	pm
Lofthouse dep.	1.30	5.00	4.45
Scar Village arr.	2.30	5.40	5.25

Tickets from the author's collection.

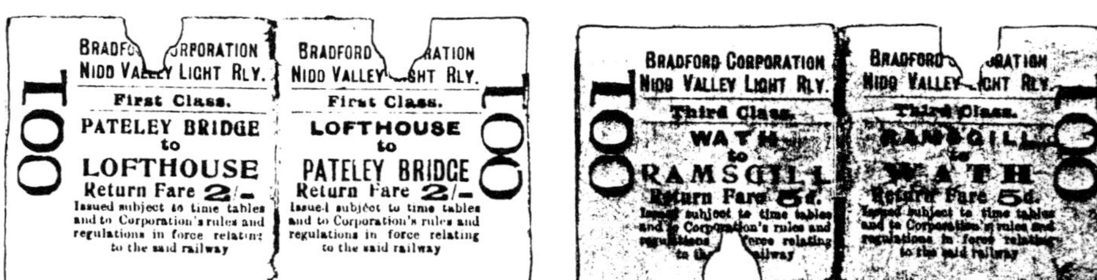

Tickets by courtesy of Premier Tickets, Leicester.

Chapter Nine

Rules and Regulations

Although the Nidd Valley Light Railway was only around six miles in length, it was worked to standards which would not be out of place on a main line railway.

The main working document was the volume of 'Rules and Regulations'. This was a dull green volume 4¼in. × 5¾in. containing 191 pages, and would appear to have been the standard issue to railways conforming to government regulations. This is suggested by the fact that none of the regulations appear to relate specifically to the Nidd Valley Light Railway, and many of them would not be applicable on such a line. Nevertheless, some of them make amusing reading:

> 200. Newspapers or other parcels must not be thrown from trains as they pass through intermediate stations, unless specifically sanctioned by the General Superintendent. Where authority has been given for parcels to be thrown off, Guards must, before throwing the parcels from the train, satisfy themselves that the platforms are clear, and Station-masters and others must warn persons who may be about to keep clear of the train.
>
> 203. Insane persons, and prisoners under the charge of police, must not be placed with other passengers, but in a separate compartment.

A printed title page was pasted on to the cover of the book, and was dated September 1907 (see *Plate B*). Each employee of the railway was issued with a copy of the above book, and was required to sign and date a declaration to the effect that he had received a copy (see *Plate C*).

A separate un-dated booklet was also issued to railway personnel. This contained 'Regulations for train signalling', and measured 4¼in. × 5½in., and contained 44 pages of operating procedures. It was printed in Bradford by William Byles & Sons Ltd, a well-known local printer (see *Plate D*).

A three-page printed leaflet, measuring 3¾in. × 5¼in. was also produced for the line, describing the bell system used in connection with the telegraph system between stations. This also appears to have been printed locally (see *Plate E*).

The railway also employed an internal telephone system, and an 8in. × 5in. card was displayed at appropriate locations. This was dated September 1907 (see *Plate F*).

On a lighter note, notices were displayed at stations forbidding smoking and spitting in station booking halls and waiting rooms. This too was printed locally, and was dated December 1907 (see *Plate G*).

Nidd Valley Light Railway.

RULES AND REGULATIONS.

*I** ______________________________

employed on the Nidd Valley Light Railway belonging to the Bradford Corporation, as ________ *at* ____________ *hereby acknowledge to have received a copy of "The Rules and Regulations for the Guidance of the Officers and Men in the service of the Bradford Corporation on the above-named Light Railway, from 12th September, 1907."*

Signature, ______________________

Dated the ______ *day of* ______________ *190*

* *Insert full name.*

To be filled up and returned to your Superior Officer.

E 915.

Plate C

Nidd Valley Light Railway.

RULES AND REGULATIONS

AND

Amended Rules and Regulations

ALSO

RULES FOR WORKING SIGNALS by the TABLET SYSTEM,

For the guidance of the Officers and Men in the employ of the Bradford Corporation on the above-named Light Railway as and from the 12th September, 1907, and each person on the Light Railway must make himself acquainted with the same, and he will be held responsible for a knowledge of and compliance therewith.

WM. THOS. CROFT,
Secretary.

Town Hall, Bradford,
September, 1907.

E 915

Plate B

BRADFORD CORPORATION

NIDD VALLEY LIGHT RAILWAY

REGULATIONS for TRAIN SIGNALLING

BRADFORD:

WM. BYLES AND SONS LTD., PRINTERS, PICCADILLY.

Plate D

Code of Terms and Regulations for TRAIN SIGNALLING BY BLOCK TELEGRAPH (1-Wire Semaphore Instruments with Two Positions) on Single Lines of Railway.

BELL SIGNALS.

	Beats on Bell.	How to be given.
Call attention	1	1.
Train entering Section	*2	2, consecutively.
Is Line Clear for Train?	4	4 consecutively.
Train out of Section, or Obstruction removed	3	2 *pause* 1.
Obstruction Danger	6	6 consecutively.
Blocking Back	6	*Inside* Home Signal—2 *pause* 4. *Outside* Home Signal—3 *pause* 3.
Stop and Examine Train	7	7 consecutively.
Cancelling "Is Line Clear" Signal or "Train entering Section" Signal	8	3 *pause* 5.
Train passed without SIDE LAMPS or Tail Lamp	9	9 consecutively **to Box in Advance.** 4 *pause* 5 **to Box in Rear.**
Train Divided	10	5 *pause* 5.
Section Clear but Station or Junction Blocked	*13	3 *pause* 5 *pause* 5.
Vehicles Running away	14	4 *pause* 5 *pause* 5.
Opening of Signal Box	15	5 *pause* 5 *pause* 5.
Testing Block Indicator and Bells	16	16 consecutively.
Closing of Signal Box	17	7 *pause* 5 *pause* 5.
Time Signal	18	8 *pause* 5 *pause* 5.
Lampman or Fog Signalman required	19	9 *pause* 5 *pause* 5.

Plate E

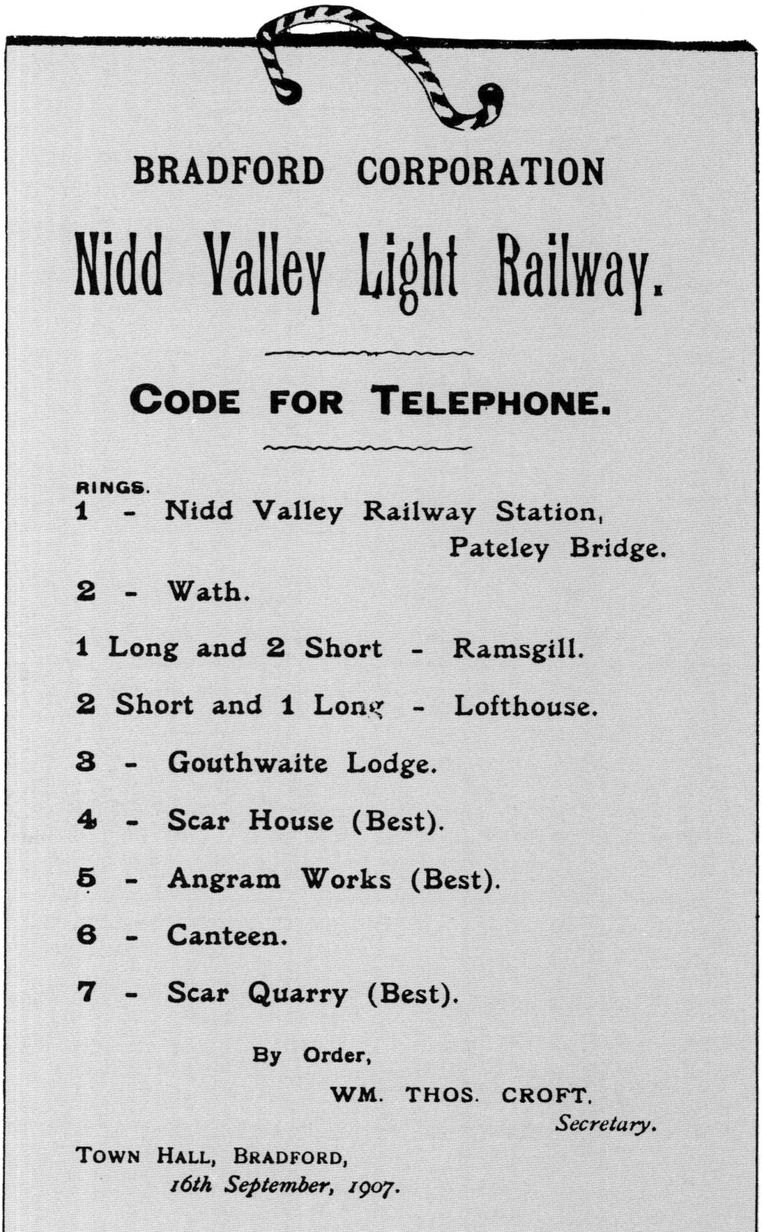

BRADFORD CORPORATION

Nidd Valley Light Railway.

CODE FOR TELEPHONE.

RINGS.

1 - Nidd Valley Railway Station, Pateley Bridge.

2 - Wath.

1 Long and 2 Short - Ramsgill.

2 Short and 1 Long - Lofthouse.

3 - Gouthwaite Lodge.

4 - Scar House (Best).

5 - Angram Works (Best).

6 - Canteen.

7 - Scar Quarry (Best).

By Order,

WM. THOS. CROFT,
Secretary.

TOWN HALL, BRADFORD,
16th September, 1907.

Plate F

NIDD VALLEY LIGHT RAILWAY.

I HEREBY GIVE NOTICE that

SMOKING & SPITTING

in the Booking Halls or Waiting Rooms of any of the Stations on the above Light Railway is

STRICTLY PROHIBITED.

By order,

WM. THOS. CROFT,
SECRETARY.

Town Hall, Bradford,
18th December, 1907.
E 1060—50 (81).

Plate G

NIDD VALLEY LIGHT RAILWAY.

PUBLIC WARNING.

Persons are WARNED NOT TO TRESPASS on this Light Railway or on any of the Lines, Stations, Works, or Premises connected therewith.

All Persons so Trespassing will be PROSECUTED for the recovery of Penalties against them.

WM. THOS. CROFT,
Secretary.

TOWN HALL, BRADFORD,
OCTOBER, 1907.
F. 1435—50 [206]

Plate H

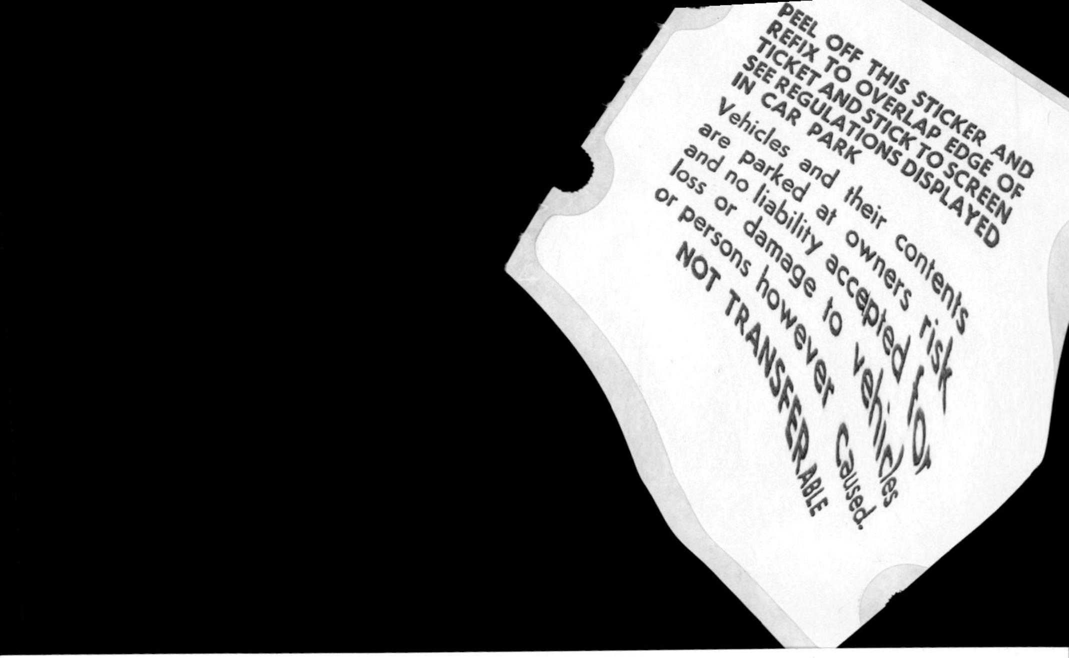

Chapter Ten

The Scar Village Site

Little has appeared in print on the subject of the workmen's communities which sprang up around the site of the many reservoirs which were constructed in the later years of the last century, and the early part of the present one. Sheffield, Manchester and Liverpool each had shanty towns on their reservoir construction sites, and all were presumably very much the same. Fortunately, quite a lot is known of the Scar House community which was constructed by Bradford Corporation to house its substantial workforce, and as it was partly served by the Nidd Valley Light Railway, its inclusion here is justified.

Before considering the Scar House 'village' in detail, it is worth looking at the location of the settlement to help to understand its existence and the number of workpeople it was built to house. Scar House 'village' was begun in October 1921, and was situated about a dozen miles from Pateley Bridge towards the head of the Nidd Valley. The 'village' at Angram Reservoir still further up the valley had been in use from 1904 to 1916, but was on a much smaller scale than its neighbour. Scar House's distance from Pateley Bridge, where the nearest shop was situated meant that the 'village' had to be virtually self-sufficient, in view of the fact that between 1,000 and 1,100 people were regularly in residence there.

Housing was of major importance on the Scar House site, where bitter winter weather had to be contended with. To begin with, many of the workmen were housed off-site in part of the workhouse at Pateley Bridge, from where they were transported free of charge by train to the reservoir site. This arrangement ended when the housing at the village was completed. Two types of housing were provided – hostels and bungalows.

The ten workmen's hostels were built of wood framing, covered on the outside with tongue and groove weatherboarding, and lined inside with matchboarding. The roofs were covered with red asbestos tiles, and surmounted with blue Staffordshire ridge tiles. Each hostel provided accommodation for 64 men, and consisted of a large kitchen, scullery, pantry, a private sitting room and bedroom for the caretaker, bathrooms, and drying rooms. Each workman was provided with a separate cubicle fitted out with a bed, chair and mirror, for which a charge of 8*d* (3½p) per night was made.

The 62 bungalows were provided for foremen and tradesmen on the site, and were of similar construction to the hostels. There were three sizes, Type A with 5 rooms at 9*s* (45p) per week; Type B with 4 rooms at 8*s* (40p) per week; and Type C with 3 rooms at 7*s* (35p) per

Scar Villas (Bungalows). Sixty-two of these bungalows were home to foremen and tradesmen at Scar House.

Courtesy Bradford Libraries & Information Service

This canteen had to provide meals for up to 1,000 men each day. Visitors dined in a separate section at one end.

Courtesy Bradford Libraries & Information Service

This Mission Hall served at both Angram and Scar House sites.

Courtesy Bradford Libraries & Information Service

Silent films provided the entertainment at Scar House, along with Saturday evening dances in the Concert Hall shown below.

Courtesy Bradford Libraries & Information Service

The hospital had served at Angram before being moved to Scar House.
Courtesy Bradford Libraries & Information Service

The village school shown here, was taken over by the West Riding County Council in 1931. *Courtesy Bradford Libraries & Information Service*

Part of the Scar House construction site, looking eastwards. *Pearce Higgins Collection, National Railway Museum, York.*

Pateley Bridge locomotive shed and water tower, with steam railcar *Hill* on the left. *Photomatic Ltd*

Locomotive *Milner* at the head of a train at Lofthouse station. *Photomatic Ltd*

Locomotive *Milner* at the head of a short train at Lofthouse. *Photomatic Ltd*

The steam railcar *Hill,* photographed at Lofthouse station. *Photomatic Ltd*

Passenger and goods trains hard at work on the steep section between Lofthouse and Scar House. The short goods train has four locomotives to work it!
Photomatic Ltd

Pateley Bridge station after the closure of the line.
LGRP, Courtesy David and Charles

Another view from the platform at Pateley Bridge some years after the closure of the line. *LGRP, Courtesy David and Charles*

week. All three types contained a separate bathroom, pantry, store-room and heating.

With such a large residential population, it was essential to have centralised catering facilities. The main canteen building consisted of one large room measuring 92ft by 80ft, and was divided into three portions. The central portion was used by the ordinary workmen, whilst the end parts were reserved for foremen and visitors respectively.

On such a desolate site as Scar House, recreational facilities were also essential. The recreation hall included a billiard room with two tables, and a separate reading room, where newspapers, magazines and books were provided free of charge. This building was built by F.T. Walker of Sheffield, and opened in 1922 at a cost of £1,525. A library service was begun on 12th February, 1923, and soon had over 450 members borrowing in excess of 5,000 books per year. The library opening hours were Monday and Friday 3.30–4.30 pm, and Monday, Wednesday and Saturday, 6.30–7.30 pm.

A concert hall measuring 92ft by 45ft was opened in September 1922, and a cinema was also provided on Tuesday and Wednesday evenings. The cinema had seating for 600 people, and the charge for viewing the silent films was 3d (1½p) at the front, and 6d (2½p) at the back. The film projection house was built of concrete to make it fire-proof, and this part of the building still stands today. On Saturday evenings, a general social gathering was held in the Concert Hall.

Outdoor pursuits were also encouraged by the provision of an allotment garden, though it is doubtful whether much would grow in such an inhospitable location! In the early 1920s, it was also suggested that a golf course and tennis courts should be added. A football team was formed, and matches were played on a pitch at Ramsgill, which was considered to be more convenient for visiting teams.

The site hospital had previously served at Angram, and had been rebuilt and altered for use at Scar House. A resident doctor and nurse were on hand to treat casualties which must have been numerous on a busy construction site like this. However, at one time, the hospital ward had only 6 beds, so perhaps serious injuries were few. It is believed that only one man lost his life during the construction of the Scar House Reservoir.

The spiritual needs of the community were met by a Mission Hall which had been bought by Bradford Corporation from the Navvy Mission Society for use at Angram. The building was still in good condition and was dismantled and moved down to Scar House, where it was re-erected near to the Concert Hall. Services were held each Sunday, and from 1922 to June 1932, a monthly parish magazine was produced called the 'Scar Village', which recorded births, marriages and deaths, plus general news about activities in the parish.

A block of six single-storey shops formed the commercial centre of the village. These were let to the firm of Marrison & Co. of Bradford, and comprised a hairdresser and newsagent, a greengrocer and fishmonger, a drapery store, butchers shop and a boot repairers. All the supplies for these shops were brought in by train over the Nidd Valley Light Railway. A sub Post Office was opened in the grocery store on 4th April, 1923, and this facility remained until 1932. In November 1926, the shops became a limited company, trading under the name of 'The Scar House Stores Ltd'. A welcome addition to the shops was the provision of a fish and chip shop, though the date of opening is not known. A separate bakery supplied the works canteen, and this was equipped with an electrically-driven plant which was capable of baking 200 loaves per hour.

The laundry building had an interesting history, for it was previously the goods sheds at Wath and Ramsgill stations. When these stations ceased to handle goods traffic in the early 1920s, the two corrugated sheds were transferred up to Scar House by train and rebuilt into a more than adequate laundry, opening for business on 10th November, 1922.

A small school was provided at Scar House, and at one time it had around 50 pupils. It was taken over by the West Riding County Council as from 1st January, 1931. A mysterious fire occurred in a classroom cupboard on 12th October, 1928, resulting in around £200 worth of damage. None of the pupils admitted causing the fire, and the matter was never solved!

A Savings Bank was opened on 28th October, 1922.

Law and order on the construction site was the responsibility of the West Riding Constabulary, although little crime seems to have been experienced. A village fire service was established with 12 men who practised their drill three nights a week, which was important in view of the large number of timber buildings on site, and the high population in a fairly restricted area.

The railway in the village consisted of a number of sidings, and a locomotive shed measuring 72ft by 30ft, complete with inspection pits. A small locomotive shed was also maintained on the north side of the valley. No proper station building existed, though a wooden-framed platform served as a terminus in this inhospitable location which was 'home' for so many people.

Chapter Eleven

The Scot Gate Ash Quarry Co. Ltd

The Scot Gate Ash Quarry Co. Ltd had no financial connection with Bradford Corporation or the Nidd Valley Light Railway. However, its proximity to the latter's terminus at Pateley Bridge, and the fact that the company's inclined tramway brought down stone which was subsequently removed over the track connecting the Nidd Valley line to the North Eastern Railway's station makes it worthy of inclusion here.

The quarry known as Scot Gate Ash is situated on the hillside to the north of Pateley Bridge, and was first worked in the 1840s. It was enlarged in the early 1870s by John and George Metcalfe of Glass-houses Mill. The Scot Gate Ash Stone Co. Ltd was incorporated in 1872, and at about this time, the inclined tramway was constructed, largely at the expense of George Metcalfe.

The line was standard gauge, and commenced at the end of the North Eastern Railway's goods yard across the road from the main station building. Leaving the sidings, the line curved to the right, and passed in front of the site of the Nidd Valley station. Shortly after this, a trailing siding on the right hand side of the line ran back along-side the unloading platform close to Millfield Street. The line started to rise here, and passed over Greenwood Road (originally called Corporation Road) on a low bridge, before the incline proper began. From here, the line was approximately 600 yards in length, terminating at the quarry some 450 feet above the town. A bridge crossed the incline taking the high road from Pateley Bridge to Wath, and not far beyond this, the line divided into a passing loop for about 100 yards, after which the tracks converged to form a three-rail interlaced section to the summit.

At the top of the incline was the winding house from which a drum 16 feet in diameter hauled wagons up and down by means of two strong steel wire ropes. In this building was an indicator showing on what part of the incline the two trucks were, this being especially useful in dark or foggy weather. There were also four levers connected by wires to switches on the rails, so that if the rope broke, or any other incident took place, the trucks could be thrown off the line at almost any part of their journey, thus avoiding loss of life or damage to property at the foot of the incline. This was an important consideration, for the line was very steep, with a gradient of 1 in 5 for much of the way, increasing to 1 in 3 near the top. The time taken for the descent of a loaded truck was 2 minutes, the empties being taken up by the weight of those coming down.

Like all industrial locations, there were accidents, though in the case of the Scot Gate quarries, these were fortunately few. As far as is

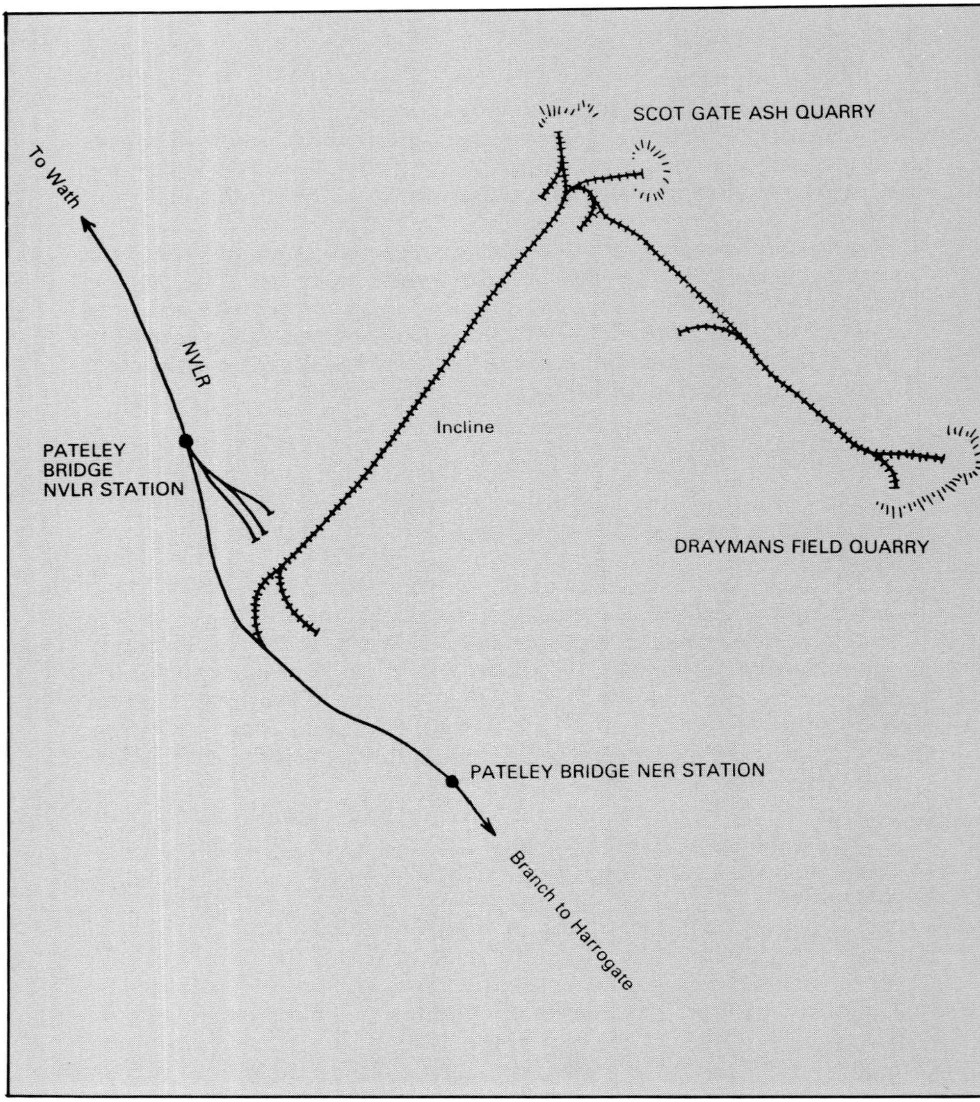

Map showing Scot Gate Ash Quarry Tramway and Nidd Valley Light Railway.

known, the tramway claimed only one victim, that being a Mr Robert Ingleby, a local man who was killed whilst crossing the rails.

The wagons used on the tramway were either those belonging to the quarry company, or to the North Eastern Railway, thus overcoming the need for transhipment at Pateley Bridge.

Beyond the winding house, the tracks fanned out, one trailing spur running back to the blacksmith's shop, whilst another ran due north into the centre of the quarry where loading platforms were situated. The third line, and by far the longest, was opened in 1891, and ran south-east along the top of the hillside to Draymans Field Quarry, some 400 yards away.

The lines inside the quarry complex were also standard gauge, and were largely horse-worked, certainly in the mid-1870s, but it is understood that at one time a small steam locomotive was also employed, but further details are not known. There were also a number of steam cranes operating in the quarry on track with a gauge of 10 feet. At one time as many as 500 men and 50 boys worked at Scot Gate, and their output resulted in three stone trains leaving Pateley Bridge each day. The quality of the stone was very high, and amongst the buildings constructed from Scot Gate stone are the National Gallery and the South Kensington Museums in London, and the present railway station and hotel in York.

During a great storm in 1892, thousands of tons of rock and earth were dislodged from the quarry, and were washed down into Pateley Bridge. Much of the inclined tramway was destroyed, and for a time it seemed that as many as 300 men would lose their jobs as a result. However, the tramway was restored, George Metcalfe paying half the cost himself, thus ensuring their jobs.

A change in the company's fortunes brought about a reduction in the workforce early this century, and by 1912, the quarries were largely disused, final closure taking place during World War I.

All that is left today of this once great complex is the track-bed of the tramway, and a few grass-covered relics in the quarry itself, and it is hard to imagine that this site was once one of the great employers of Nidderdale.

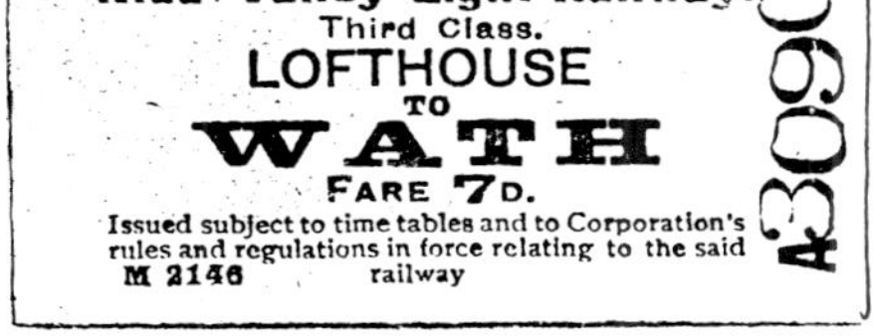
BRADFORD CORPORATION
Nidd Valley Light Railway.
Third Class.
LOFTHOUSE
TO
WATH
FARE 7D.
Issued subject to time tables and to Corporation's rules and regulations in force relating to the said railway
M 2146
A3090

Ticket by courtesy of Premier Tickets, Leicester.

Chapter Twelve

Narrow Gauge in the Nidd Valley

As one might expect with large construction sites, several of the contractors engaged on work in the Nidd Valley employed narrow gauge systems to assist in their work. Two contractors are known to have operated narrow gauge lines at three locations in the valley.

John Best & Sons Ltd of Edinburgh won the contract for the construction of the Angram Reservoir. Work commenced in August 1904, and was completed in 1919. For the commencement of the project, a 3ft gauge railway was built from a temporary station at Syke's Brow, situated about half a mile south of Lofthouse, and extending some 7 miles to the construction site at Angram. The line was certainly in operation by the middle of July 1904, when on the 14th a large party of civic officials visited Nidderdale to witness the cutting of the first sod of the Nidd Valley Light Railway, and then travelled along Best's narrow gauge railway to inaugurate the construction of Angram Reservoir. This special train consisted of about 15 'navvy waggons' fitted with seats, and hauled by two locomotives. It is not possible to identify the locomotives from photographic evidence, but of the two following locomotives, the first is known to have worked on this line, and in the case of the second, it seems a strong possibility.

Angram. Hudswell, Clarke 0–4–0ST (Works No. 397). Built 1892 for the Newcastle & Gateshead Water Company for use at their Whittle Dean site, and named *Whittle Dean.* Outside cylinders 10in. × 16in. Driving wheels 2ft 9in. Sold to Best's for the Angram contract, and re-named *Angram.* It was later used by Best's on the Delph Reservoir contract, near Oldham, where it was numbered 21, though retaining the name *Angram.* By 1918, it had been sold to Nott, Brodie & Co. Ltd for use on the Blaen-y-Cwm Reservoir project at Beaufort, where it was named *Reindeer.* It was retained on this contract until 1924, when it passed to Barnsley Corporation, by whom it was used at the Scout Dike and Royd Moor Works, and carried the name *Barnsley.* It subsequently passed to Richard Baillie at Ladybower Reservoir around 1936, and is believed to have been dismantled in 1938.

(? name). Hunslet Engine Co. 0–4–0ST (Works No. 759). Built 1901 for the Baldwin Reservoir Tramway on the Isle of Man, and then named *Ardwhallin.* In May 1905, it was sold to Tynemouth Corporation for use on the Fontburn Reservoir, and re-named *Tynemouth.* Best's acquired it in May 1909 and used it on Oldham Corporation's Delph Reservoir project. J.I.C. Boyd's book *The Isle of Man Railway,* published in 1962 (Oakwood) suggests that the locomotive may then have been used on Sheffield Corporation's reservoir contract at Angram, but this is presumably an error for Bradford Corporation. No further details of its use are known.

By 1906, the line between Syke's Brow and Angram had been relaid to standard gauge, the portion between Syke's Brow and Lofthouse being incorporated into the Nidd Valley Light Railway, and that beyond Lofthouse being used solely by contractors engaged on the Angram, and later Scar House reservoir projects. What became of the locomotives is not known, but they were presumably used on temporary tracks laid around the Angram site.

Morrison & Mason of Glasgow are known to have worked two narrow gauge systems in Upper Nidderdale.

The first was centred at Heathfield, a tiny hamlet to the west of Wath. Here in 1894 was established a narrow gauge railhead in connection with the construction of the aqueduct which was to carry water from Angram Reservoir, and then later from Scar House, to the taps of Bradford. It is understood that a number of 3ft gauge locomotives were used on this work, but further details are not known.

The second site was at Scar House Reservoir. Little is known of this operation except that a narrow gauge 0–4–0ST with the contractor's name along the tank sides was used. A small number of four-wheeled trucks were at one time fitted with benches for the carriage of passengers.

It is possible that other narrow gauge lines existed on the reservoir sites from time to time, and it has also been suggested that some of the quarries had 3ft gauge lines, though these may have been solely for moving quantities of stone by hand to the standard gauge tracks, to be conveyed down to the construction sites.

In addition to the narrow gauge lines worked by the contractors, Bradford Corporation Waterworks Department also operated a small narrow gauge system at Scar House Reservoir. This was of 2ft gauge, though little is known about the operations. There is believed to have been a 6½ ton Simplex diesel built in 1932, and possibly numbered 71. It is known to have been transferred to the Chellow Heights Waterworks in Haworth Road, Bradford after use at Scar House. In its new home, it was found to be too wide and too heavy, and it was moved again, this time to Hewenden Reservoir, near Denholme, not far from the Great Northern branch from Bradford to Keighley. It is believed to have been used here for only a short time during repairs to the reservoir, and was subsequently sold by the Corporation, though no further trace is known of its whereabouts. The only other evidence of this system comes from a 6in. to 1 mile Ordnance Survey map dated 1956, which shows a narrow gauge line running westwards from Scar Dam along the northern shore of Scar House Reservoir towards Angram, but terminating about ¼ mile before reaching Angram. Part of the track is shown as being extant in 1956, though the section nearest Scar House is shown merely as 'track of old tramway'.

Bradford Corporation.

NIDD VALLEY LIGHT RAILWAY

Local Rates and Charges for Animals

By MERCHANDISE TRAINS.

DISTANCE.	STATIONS.	1.		2.		3.		4.		5.		6.	
		For every Horse, Mule or other Beast of Draught or Burden but the Consignor will be required to provide his own Truck		For every Ox, Cow, Bull or head of Neat Cattle the following Charges, with a minimum charge of 5/		For every Animal of the several Classes named in Columns 1 and 2, conveyed in a separate carriage by direction of the Consignor or from necessity		For each Truck containing any consignment by the same person of such number of Oxen, Cows, Neat Cattle, Calves, Sheep, Goats or Pigs, as may reasonably be carried in a truck of 13 feet 6 inches in length, inside measurement		15 feet 6 inches in length, inside measurement.		18 feet in length, inside measurement.	
		s.	d.	s.	d.	s.	d.	s.	d.	s.	d.	s.	d.
Under 3 miles	PATELEY to WATH	2	7	1	9	6	10	4	10	5	8	6	6
„ 4¼ „	„ „ RAMSGILL	2	11	2	0	7	7	5	7	6	7	7	6
„ 6 „	„ „ LOFTHOUSE	3	6	2	6	8	9	6	9	7	10	9	0
„ 3 „	WATH to PATELEY	2	7	1	9	6	10	4	10	5	8	6	6
	„ „ RAMSGILL												
„ 4¾ „	„ „ LOFTHOUSE	3	1	2	1	7	11	5	11	6	11	7	11
„ 4¼ „	RAMSGILL to PATELEY	2	11	2	0	7	7	5	7	6	7	7	6
	„ „ WATH												
„ 3 „	„ „ LOFTHOUSE	2	7	1	9	6	10	4	10	5	8	6	6
	LOFTHOUSE to RAMSGILL												
„ 4¾ „	„ „ WATH	3	1	2	1	7	11	5	11	6	11	7	11
„ 6 „	„ „ PATELEY	3	6	2	6	8	9	6	9	7	10	9	0

THE RATES in the above Table do not include any charge for Cleansing Trucks.

Where the Corporation are required to cleanse and do cleanse Trucks, a Charge not exceeding One Shilling per Truck may be made in addition to the Rates in this Table.

BY ORDER,

WM. THOS. CROFT,

SECRETARY.

TOWN HALL, BRADFORD,

September, 1907.

Chapter Thirteen

The Line Today

So much for the past, but what of the Nidd Valley Light Railway today? All four station buildings are still standing, and are in use as private houses. The one at Pateley Bridge takes a bit of finding as it is surrounded by modern houses, but the old railway station gives itself away by its position at right angles to the track-bed, and is easily identified because of its architecture. The station buildings at Wath and Ramsgill are particularly attractive houses, whilst the Lofthouse building now serves as a shop and cafe also.

Unfortunately it is not possible to walk along the track-bed for the entire length of the railway. The Pateley Bridge to Wath section is more or less intact but to reach it one has to take a public footpath parallel to the river for a short way before the old railway comes into sight. From here it is possible to walk along the track-bed, past the site of the locomotive and carriage sheds, almost to Wath station.

Beyond Wath, the track-bed is available as a footpath as far as the dam wall at Gouthwaite Reservoir, beyond which one is obliged to follow the hillside because the line ran so close to the reservoir that the land is now owned by the Yorkshire Water Authority. Between Ramsgill and Lofthouse, the track-bed is available as a public footpath.

From Lofthouse to Angram it is possible to walk along the private road which was constructed at the same time as the railway. Until about 1974, this section was not accessible to the public, but since then, the Yorkshire Water Authority has allowed the public access to this picturesque stretch, and has landscaped parts of it with picnic areas, and provided a car park and toilets at Scar House. The tunnel can clearly be seen, but it is bricked up to prevent mishaps. At Scar House, the foundations of some of the buildings can be seen, but there is no evidence of the railway.

Back at Pateley Bridge, the inclined tramway to the Scot Gate Ash Quarries can be seen, and the quarries themselves make a pleasant walk.

The best reminder of the Nidd Valley Light Railway can be found in the Nidderdale Museum close to the centre of Pateley Bridge. Here a comprehensive selection of photographs of the railway and the reservoir construction sites is on display. The museum is open for visitors on Sunday afternoons, and is well worth a visit.

Chapter Fourteen

The Nidd Valley in Retrospect

Now that we have reached the end of the story of the Nidd Valley Light Railway, it is worth considering the achievements made by the line during its period of operation, and to consider what might have developed if fate, or perhaps railway history, had taken a different course.

Probably its main achievement was that it was the only municipally-owned light railway ever built in this country, which is in itself a distinction. Other local authorities have operated railways in connection with waterworks, gas works, docks etc., but none has ever run a passenger service for the general public.

It was probably also unique in that two railway systems shared the same tracks, for the trains of the Nidd Valley Light Railway were interspersed throughout their existence with those of reservoir construction trains hauled by contractors' locomotives on both freight and passenger workings.

During its twenty-two years of passenger service, the Nidd Valley Light Railway gave valiant service to the people of Upper Nidderdale, and it also had a profound effect on the developing of a new industry, that of tourism. Many thousands of Bradfordians travelled over the line to see what their far-sighted civic leaders had created in this remote dale in the way of new waterworks. And still they come today, though now by private car to marvel at Scar House and Angram, and Gouthwaite.

For twenty-nine years, the Nidd Valley Light Railway also served the City of Bradford, and indirectly its citizens, by enabling the great reservoirs to be built, for without the line it is doubtful if the scheme could have been completed.

But if, in those far-off days at the turn of the century things had developed in other ways, we might just have finished reading a completely different railway history.

If Power & Traction Ltd had succeeded with their scheme back in 1901, their resulting 2ft 6in. gauge railway might eventually have resembled the Leek & Manifold Valley Light Railway or the Welshpool & Llanfair Caereinion Light Railway, both of which closed to passengers in the 1930s, though the latter has survived in preserved form.

The change of gauge to 3ft in 1903 could have made Bradford Corporation the proud owners of a system like the Southwold Railway, or the more elaborate lines of the Isle of Man or Ireland. These latter systems survived much longer than their narrower gauge counterparts, and a remnant of the Manx system still survives as a popular tourist attraction.

Even as a standard gauge line, the Nidd Valley Light Railway might have had a different future, especially if it could have been taken over by Colonel Stephens, and added to his empire of fascinating light railways, instead of being allowed to close by Bradford Corporation. However, the Colonel was no doubt considering his retirement when the fortunes of the Nidd Valley were beginning to change.

The electrification proposals of the early 1920s could have created an entirely new feel to the line, but in so doing would have lost the unique character which light railways possessed. It is hard to imagine what the railway would have looked like with overhead wires and electric locomotives, but it would certainly have had the distinction of being Britain's first electric light railway.

It is probably fair to say that if the North Eastern Railway had acquired the Nidd Valley line in 1929 when it was offered to them, then it might have still been in existence to this day. The Pateley Bridge to Lofthouse section could have become an extension to the branch from Harrogate to Pateley Bridge, and had this occurred, it might still have had a passenger service until 1951. Goods traffic on the NER line to Pateley Bridge ceased in 1964, by which time the preservation movement was beginning, and what an ideal candidate the Nidd Valley Light Railway would have been, but alas this was not to be.

However, we should be grateful for the existence, no matter how short, of the Nidd Valley Light Railway, for it brought to the beautiful Yorkshire Dales that feeling of independence and character which was becoming rarer with the merging of the smaller British railways into a more standardised network.

In over 20 years of operation, there must have been countless tales of happenings, amusing or otherwise, but sadly, few have survived to this day. Maybe the residents of Pateley Bridge were not always pleased to see hoardes of thirsty navvies streaming from the station, and crowding into the public houses, but they certainly kept the publicans busy! The noon train from Scar House to Pateley Bridge on a Saturday was a favourite with the workmen. Four locomotives seem to have been regular performers on this particular trip, *Gadie*, *Illingworth*, *Kitchener* and *Haig*. It was customary for the driver to give a toot on the whistle to indicate that departure was in one minute, and there would be a mad scramble to get on board for the trip down to civilisation. Getting the workers out of the pubs was another matter! Once again, a blast on the whistle was used to summon the men back to the train, and woe betide anyone who missed it! A twelve-mile walk faced them.

It was on one of these Saturday trips that a pig suddenly ran across the track in front of *Gadie*, and was killed. A near riot broke out when the navvies found out what had happened, as they wanted the driver to stop the train and go back and collect the poor dead animal, so that they could have pork for supper!

There were equally amusing tales recounted in the Angram and Scar House villages. Amongst them is the story of the man who wanted his own house. As we have seen earlier, the majority of the workmen were housed in large hostels with little peace and privacy. One day, a vacancy occurred at one of the self-contained houses, and a grim-looking navvy applied at the office. "I want the house, you see, because in the hostel I have to say 'please, this' and 'thank you, that'. I want my own house so that I can shout to the wife 'Gimme summat to eat', and tell everybody else to shut up. I want to be master in my own house". Sadly, he never was, for the house was given to someone else!

But what of the future? There have already been several cases of lines being re-born, sometimes as narrow gauge or even miniature lines, using the track-bed of their former standard gauge counterparts. Two examples in Wales immediately spring to mind, these being the Bala Lake Railway, and the Brecon Mountain Railway. Is it too late to think that we may one day be able to travel again along part of the Nidd Valley Light Railway, and go back in time, in our minds, and visualise *Milner* or *Gadie* at the head of a train to Lofthouse?

Author's Collection

Sources, Bibliography and Acknowledgements

Considering its importance in railway history, surprisingly little has appeared in print about the Nidd Valley Light Railway. The basis of my original booklet, published in 1972 was a number of articles contained in various railway periodicals, including the following:

Bradford Corporation Nidderdale Light Railway. *The Locomotive Magazine*, 15th February, 1906, pp.19–20.

Bradford Corporation's railway in the Nidd Valley. *The Locomotive*, 14th September, 1929, pp.282–284.

Herbert, A.P. The Nidd Valley Light Railway. *Railway Magazine*, Vol.60, No.360, June 1927, pp.463–466.

Potter, G.W.J. The Nidd Valley Light Railway: a successful municipal undertaking. *Railway Magazine*, Vol.28, No.166, April 1911, pp.313–317.

Rawlings, I. An English municipal railway. *Railway & Travel Monthly*, Vol.10, No.60, April 1915, pp.230–234.

In more recent times, accounts of the line have appeared in:

Hird, H. *Bradford in history*. Author, 1968, pp.178–189.

Hoole, K. *Railways in the Yorkshire Dales*. Dalesman Books, 1975, pp.67–77.

Redman, R.N. *Railway byways in Yorkshire*. Dalesman Books, 1979, pp.14–16/33–34.

Further useful information was obtained from old editions of Ordnance Survey maps, and the files of local newspapers, including the *Yorkshire Post*, and the *Yorkshire Observer*. Periodicals such as *The Engineer* and *The Dalesman* have also provided useful information.

By far the most useful sources have been the Minutes and Accounts of Bradford City Council, and the weighty correspondence files of the Bradford Corporation Waterworks Department, which are now preserved by the West Yorkshire Archive Service at its Bradford office.

Interesting background material on the history of Nidderdale has been gleaned from a number of works, including:

Jennings, B. (editor). *A history of Nidderdale*, written by the Pateley Bridge Local History Tutorial Class, and published by the Advertiser Press, Huddersfield, 1967.

Speight, H. *Nidderdale from Nun Monkton to Whernside*. 1906.

Speight, H. *Upper Nidderdale, with the Forest of Knaresborough*. 1906.

Whitehead, T. *Illustrated guide to Nidderdale*. 1932.

During the compilation of this book, I have received help from several people, to whom I extend my thanks.

To David James and Ian Mason of the West Yorkshire Archive Service for unearthing dusty files from their basement,

To Miss E.M. Willmott, the Specialist Librarian for Local Studies at Bradford Reference Library for allowing me to reproduce the illustrations of the Scar Village site,

and to the late Mr Tommy Garth of Summerbridge, for his helpful letter and information following the publication of my earlier booklet on the railway.

Nidd Valley Light Railway

Chronology

1st May, 1862	Pateley Bridge branch of the North Eastern Railway opened.
30th March, 1901	Power & Traction Ltd granted permission to build a narrow gauge railway from Pateley Bridge to Lofthouse.
1st March, 1904	Bradford Corporation took over powers to construct the Nidd Valley Light Railway.
14th July, 1904	Bradford Corporation began work on the Nidd Valley Light Railway.
24th July, 1907	Board of Trade inspection.
11th September, 1907	Nidd Valley Light Railway officially opened, with public service commencing the following day.
11th June, 1929	Decision taken to close the railway.
31st December, 1929	Nidd Valley Light Railway closes to passengers.
16th June, 1937	Sale of Nidd Valley Light Railway stock and construction equipment began.

The Reservoirs of the Nidd Valley

The reservoirs of the upper part of the Nidd Valley are so closely connected with the history of the Nidd Valley Light Railway that some further information may be of interest.

Gouthwaite Reservoir

Construction began:	30th September, 1893
Contractor:	John Best & Sons Ltd.
Work completed:	6th November, 1901
Total cost:	£240,000
Capacity:	1,565 million gallons
Area:	327 acres
Height above sea level:	446 feet

Angram Reservoir

Construction began:	14th July, 1904
Contractor:	John Best & Sons Ltd.
Work completed:	1919
Estimated cost:	£400,000
Capacity:	1,042 million gallons
Area:	84.75 acres
Height above sea level:	1187.5 feet

Scar House Reservoir

Construction began:	5th October, 1921
Contractor:	John Best & Sons Ltd.
Work completed:	7th September, 1936
Total cost:	£2,200,000
Capacity:	2,200 million gallons
Area:	172 acres
Height above sea level:	1054.5 feet